# MONTANA WILDLIFE

NUMBER 3

BY ROBERT C. (BERT) GILDART
WITH JAN WASSINK

Published By

## MONTANA MAGAZINE, INC.

Helena, Montana

Rick Graetz, Publisher
Mark Thompson, Editor
Carolyn Cunningham, Managing Editor

# PREFACE

Montana has staged some of the world's most dazzling wildlife pageants: bison hooves shaking the earth, a gaggle of geese winging across a moonlit sky, the lunge of a grizzly overtaking an elk. Such spectacles were common a hundred years ago. The wonder of it is we still find them in Montana today! And, if guarded jealously, our cornucopia of wildlife will continue to spill into every corner of the state.

Be aware, however, that our grizzly walks the edge of extinction. And although we may still see thundering herds of bison in their last refuge, their numbers are miniscule in comparison to yesterday. If taken for granted, other wild creatures will disappear as swiftly and surely.

The purpose of this book then, beyond offering the simple pleasure of picture-gazing, is to foster in Montanans a protective feeling for wildlife — and an interest in its future. With the hope that coming generations might thrill as we do to the beauty of it all, we dedicate this book to our children: David and Angie Gildart, Kip and Chad Wassink.

## ACKNOWLEDGMENTS

The authors would like to express their gratitude to the following for assistance in completing this book: Smithsonian Magazine for permission to reprint the grizzly bear article which appeared in the August '81 issue; Mike Aderhold, and other employees of Montana's Department of Fish, Wildlife and Parks stationed in Kalispell, for time and directional advice; and particularly Dr. Robert Martinka, also of the Montana Department of Fish, Wildlife and Parks, who graciously agreed to review and comment on sections of this book. Additionally, the following helped in other essential but unsolicited ways: Dar Wassink, Mark and Barbara Thompson, and Brig. Gen. and Mrs. Robert C. Gildart.

Montana Magazine Inc., Publisher
Box 5630, Helena, Mt. 59604
ISBN 0-938314-04-1

*Wolverine*

*Raccoon*

*Ring-necked Pheasant*

*Grizzly Bear*

*Hummingbird*

*Mountain Goat*

ox

Bull Elk

White-Faced Ibis

Canadian Lynx

Bison Bull

# CONTENTS

## THE AUTHORS

R. C. (Bert) Gildart is a contributing editor to Montana Magazine. His work has appeared in Smithsonian Institute, Sierra Club and National Park Service publications, as well as in Field & Stream, Natural History and other magazines.

Jan Wassink, a contributing editor to Montana Magazine, is a wildlife biologist and free-lance writer. He is the creator of wildlife audio-visual products for New York publishers. He has been published in Bowhunter Magazine, Archery, and Ranger Rick's nature magazine.

4

# HISTORY AND DECLINE OF MONTANA WILDLIFE

In 1854 a titled Irishman by the name of George Gore assembled a retinue of 43 men whose sole purpose was to venture into Montana and, as he put it, "Gather a little meat." One year later, they appeared at Ft. Union boasting of having killed 105 bears, 2,000 buffalo and innumerable elk, antelope and deer. Virtually all had been left rotting on the plains. Crow Indians and Indian Agent Col. A. J. Vaughn were furious. The former responded by driving off all horses belonging to the Gore party. The latter responded by documenting the extent of the slaughter providing journalists in Montana territory with sufficient justification to label Sir Gore as "the prize winning game hog of all time."

In the wake of the massive slaughter and mismanagement of wildlife that followed, it is irrelevant whether Gore is deserving of this reputation. What is significant is the fact that less than a century and a half ago scientists say that Montana was endowed with more wildlife numbers than Africa's Serengeti Plains. So vast were the herds of wildlife that wandered over the Western grasslands that virtually every explorer and hunter who possessed the education and inclination and traveled through the area that was to become Montana was motivated to enter sightings in his journals. Wrote Captain Lewis in 1804 in the most heralded of the early-day journals, "The whole face of the country was covered with herds of buffalo, elk and antelope." At the time, the Lewis and Clark

*Opposite Page: Laws to protect Montana game were not enacted until 1872. Any form and quantity of wild animals could be taken.*

Expedition was passing above the mouth of the Yellowstone.

About 60 years later wildlife still rambled across Montana's plains and occasionally even choked her rivers. Wrote James Mills Hanson of a trip to Fort Benton as late in the century as 1866: ". . . the buffalo became so thick in the river that the boat could not move, and the engine had to be stopped. In front, the channel was blocked by their huge shaggy bodies, and in their struggles, they beat against the sides and stern."

No doubt about it, Montana was once a haven for wildlife, but about the same time Hanson was recording his observations several events were beginning that would have a more dramatic effect on big game resources than the slaughter left in the wake of Gore's expedition and the many others who were similarly disposed.

The discovery of gold and the 1862 Homestead Act caused thousands of easterners to move westward in search of free land on the prairies. Many came to Montana on steamboats, which by then were navigating the upper Missouri as far north as Great Falls, and which were on the Yellowstone by the mid 1800s. Others drove the first herds of cattle to the territory in the early 1860s and then stayed. Within a few short years, virtually millions of acres of big game habitat had been converted to farmland or used by cattle. Meanwhile, hides continued as a lucrative source of income for many. In 1876, Fort Benton sent 80,000 buffalo hides to the St. Louis market. Further helping to deplete the

wildlife resource was the value placed on other hides. In Montana, deer hides were used as a source of legal tender, having a value of 50 cents each.

Elk presented a unique example of exploitation. Unlike other members of the deer family, elk possess a pair of ivory-like canine teeth or "buglers" in the upper jaw. In the early 1900s, coutless elk were shot just for their teeth. These teeth were especially cherished as fobs for pocket watches and by members of the Benevolent Order of the Elk. Market value for a pair of such teeth was $75.

During the period of exploitation, many western states began following the example of their eastern predcessors. Montana was no exception, and by the late 1800s, laws were being enacted for the protection of game. In 1872, legislation closed the hunting season on buffalo, moose, elk, deer, bighorn sheep, mountain goats and hares. In 1895, the Montana legislature authorized the first Fish and Game Board which in turn established a season and quota on big game. That year the law limited hunters to eight deer, eight bighorn sheep, eight mountain goats, eight antelope, two moose and two elk. No license was required and wouldn't be until 1905, when residents were required to pay $1.

During those years little was understood about ecology or wildlife management and, though the state was attempting to protect game and enforce established laws with wardens, apparently their positions were established more on the basis of local politics than on the basis of enthusiastic protection. If a warden's phi-

a

The state's first game quotas were established in 1895. (a) Grizzly prize near Browning, 1890s. (b) Same place, Bighorn sheep. (c) Grizzlies taken for hides also in the Browning area, 1890s. Opposite Page: Photo caption reads "Just a few of the best."

b

c

losophy differed from that of a politician, out that person went.

Not only was early-day enforcement something of a paper tiger, it was also embryonic in its scientific approach. Practiced without the benefit or knowledge of sound wildlife principles, it was doomed to ultimate failure primarily because of two incorrect assumptions: 1) The only important drain on any wildlife population was due to guns and predators; and 2) if wildlife numbers were low or absent, all that was needed was to plant farm-reared wildlife, control predators and close hunting seasons.

Perhaps the most controversial of these incorrect assumptions concerned predator control and it was practiced with thoroughness throughout the state. Even Glacier and Yellowstone Parks, established to preserve and protect all forms of wildlife, attempted to control predators. For the Park Service, the decree went out to both Glacier and Yellowstone from the highest authorities. Wrote Horace Albright, acting Director of the National Park Service on November 8, 1918: ". . . As I advised you, earlier, every ranger on your force must devote himself to the hunting and killing of predatory animals . . . they must actively engage in the extermination of the carnivorous species that are taking such a heavy toll of wild animal life in the park . . ."

This exerpt expresses an attitude that had existed since the inception of Yellowstone National Park in 1892, continued with the establishment of the prevailing attitude of the Park Service toward predators until the early 1930s. During these years, it was believed parks should protect "good animals" and destroy "bad animals."

Animals in this latter category initially were the wolf, included the lynx, bobcat, red fox, badger, mink, weasel, fisher, otter and marten. In Yellowstone, even white pelicans were reduced in numbers on the grounds that trout needed protection. Understanding more about the "balance of nature," and the vital role predators play in maintaining this balance, our hindsight seems particularly keen. But, in the early days, time had not provided the lessons that would so dramatically demonstrate the essential function of predators. A few tragedies were needed before the lesson would be learned.

One of the tragedies occurred on the Kaibab Plateau in Arizona. Here, land-use practices were changing. Cattle, sheep and horses began competing for the available plant food. But equally as significant, virtually every type of predator was being eliminated. These

a

(a) Hunting party on Magpie Gulch near Helena, 1889. (b) Coyote and beaver furs from the Judith River country.

b

*Brown the wolfer, Fallon area.*

Park Service in 1931, stated in the Journal of Mammalogy, "The National Park Service believes that predatory animals have a real place in nature, and that all animal life should be kept inviolate within the parks. As a consequence . . . predatory animals are to be considered as an integral part of the wildlife protected within national parks and no widespread campaigns of destruction are to be practiced . . ." Today, this is still the fundamental conclusion reached from those events from more than a half century ago, though it is also recognized that land-use practices also must be monitored. Some of today's biologists also suspect that the competition from cattle and sheep introduced onto the Kaibab during those years may have played a more significant role than has been recognized.

Another tragic example closer to home occurred with the northern Yellowstone elk herd that traditionally had wintered along the Yellowstone River in what is now Montana. When this area was taken over for agriculture and domestic livestock production, the elk were no longer welcome on their historic winter range. In turn, the elk were intolerant of the new civilization and wintered on marginal, often snow-covered, winter range near the Park boundary. All hunting was prohibited in the Park in 1883 and was controlled outside the Park by the state. By 1914 the herd had multiplied to the point where the remaining marginal winter range was overstocked with about 35,000 elk spending the winter around the Park boundary. Malnutrition and some starvation had been observed each winter, and during the winter of 1919-1920, about 14,000 elk died of starvation.

Many other Montana game ranges also were in jeopardy due to alteration of habitat by domestic livestock. Other problem areas traditionally recognized as big-game winter areas were observed during the '30s on the Sun River, South Fork of the Flathead, Gallatin, Little Belts and Madison. To help arrive at solutions to the problem, colleges began offering courses in wildlife management. In 1939, the first degree in wildlife technology was granted at the University of Montana in Missoula. Armed with new knowledge, biologists have re-established wildlife in many of their former haunts and learned over the past 40 years how to manage animals and habitat in such a way that conflicts of propriety have been diminished.

Today, wildlife exists in Montana for the sportsman, nature lover and photographer. Though no longer as abundant as the days when game-hog Gore hired his army of men with their 112 horses, 12 yoke of cattle, six wagons, 21 cats and 14 dogs and set out to "gather a little meat," wildlife has become one of Montana's most attractive and lucrative of resources.

practices initiated the drama that eventually would alter the thinking of many wildlife managers who previously had agreed with the philosophy of complete predator control.

As in Montana, war was declared on virtually all predators. At first, the practice of controlling predators appeared to be a magnificent success. Deer numbers increased. In less than ten years, the Kaibab herd doubled and, in 1918, numbers were estimated at 15,000. By 1922, deer in this same area exceeded 20,000; by 1923, 30,000 deer were on an area of 700,000 acres.

At that point, it was obvious that a different approach to wildlife management was required. Virtually all the food was gone, and erosion was rampant. There was no vegetation left to hold the soil, and deer began to die of starvation. Literally thousands of deer died with bloated stomach, hollowed eyes and prominent ribs. A more prolonged period of suffering could not be imagined; the lesson was there — the lesson of the Kaibab — the lesson that animal populations that have lived together are better when left to their own devices. Finally, wildlife managers went on record to that effect. Horace Albright, Director of the National

*Opposite Page: Hunting and fishing are two of Montana's major industries, and environmentally clean ones at that. Horse packer returning from the Bob Marshall Wilderness.*

*Above: Funds from the Pittman-Robertson Act provided for the re-establishment of wildlife throughout the state through a live-trapping program. Though transplanting is not practiced as frequently today, the program continues as is illustrated by the 1979 helicopter transplant of sheep from Flathead Lake's Wildhorse Island.*

# EVOLUTION OF WILDLIFE MANAGEMENT

Pick up a copy of virtually any national outdoor magazine and invariably Montana's wildlife provides substance for a feature story. "Montana Hunting Best in the West," or, "Backpack for Glacier Trout," herald one or more of the big three sporting magazines. So how did wildlife in the state ever recover from the lows of the early 1900s to such an extent that hunting and fishing are now praised in such laudatory terms?

Perhaps the greatest single reason Montana wildlife has rebounded to its present level is the passage in 1937 of the Federal Aid in Wildlife Restoration Act better known as the Pittman-Robertson Act. This law allocated to the state fish and wildlife agencies receipts from an 11 percent excise tax on sporting firearms and ammunition for the purpose of wildlife restoration and management. To qualify for assistance, the states had to pledge all hunting and fishing license funds to conservation purposes. Before that time, it was common practice for state legislature to divert income from hunting and fishing licenses for schools, highways and other public works.

Montana didn't qualify for these funds until 1941. At the same time, jurisdiction for setting all hunting seasons and regulations was transferred from the state legislature to the Fish and Game Commission.

Since 1941 the game management program has operated primarily on Federal P-R funds which support 75 percent of the cost of approved projects. Matching funds from state hunting license sales provide the other 25 percent of the cost.

Some critics of the funding program argue that because hunters carry the burden of wildlife conservation, the state agencies favor game species in their programs and ignore non-hunted species. But most serious bird watchers know that some of the best birding is found on state wildlife management areas and refuges. Waterfowl management areas provide food and cover for a host of non-game species, ranging from marsh wrens to ospreys and eagles.

One manner in which funds from the P-R program could be used was in a trapping and transplanting program. This program has proved highly successful and, beginning in 1941, a number of mountain goats were transplanted into unoccupied habitat as were sheep and beaver. The fisher, another fur bearer, was re-established in portions of northwestern Montana through transplants occurring in 1959. In addition,

11

more than 6,000 elk have been transplanted into Montana areas since the first release in 1910. From 1941 to 1970, 4,140 elk were transplanted. Most were trapped and hauled from Yellowstone National Park and released in many areas throughout the state. Today, nearly all suitable range is inhabited, so elk transplanting is no longer an important program in the state.

The P-R funds also have been used for land acquisition and development of important wildlife areas. Freezeout Lake, Fox Lake, Ninepipes and Pablo Reservoirs are examples. Today, the total area of lands owned or controlled by the Montana Department of Fish, Wildlife and Parks stands at 321,071 acres.

Considering only those animals that are hunted, the benefits of the P-R program are illustrated dramatically by the steady increase in sheer numbers. Waterfowl have increased as have deer, elk, moose and pronghorn antelope.

One way of assessing these increases is through hunter harvests. Between 1950 and 1955, the total number of deer harvested by hunters doubled. Similarly, during the same period, elk harvests improved by 25 percent.

Seasons too reopened. After 50 years of closure, moose hunting was reopened in 1945. During the same mid-century period, more liberalized seasons also were reinstituted on goats, sheep, bears, pronghorn antelope and upland game birds. In addition, two new species, chukar and Merriam's turkey were added to Montana's huntable game birds during the late 1950s. Wild turkeys were hunted in 1958, just four years after the first turkey introduction.

Although not always a part of the P-R program, another attempt to bring back herds of big game was made by the creation of wildlife refuges. In 1933, the total number of trumpeter swans south of Canada was reduced to 69 on Red Rock Lakes and Yellowstone National Park in Montana. Since that year, when Red Rocks Lakes were declared a national wildlife refuge to protect the swans from irresponsible people and to protect the swan's habitat from intrusion, the population has responded well.

Another such refuge was the National Bison Range in Moiese. Here, big game has prospered and, as populations reached or exceeded carrying capacity, excess animals were transplanted to areas where the species had been extirpated. Today, buffalo throughout the country are estimated at 6,000 with all available range considered to be fully stocked. Many of these buffalo have been transplanted from a refuge in Montana. The creation of this refuge forms one of the conservation milestones in the Americas.

a

b

*(a) Tyson Planz of the Bowdoin Wildlife Refuge releases a banded goose.*

*(b) Man-made goose platform is one of many that has helped to substantially increase productivity of geese on the CMR Wildlife Refuge.*

*(c) Montana's Red Rocks Lake Refuge was a major contributor to saving the Trumpeter Swan, shown here, which faced extinction.*

c

a

b

(a) Sun River Game Range has become nationally famous and provides essential winter range for the area's elk.

(b) Elk along Gibbon River, Yellowstone National Park.

(c) Glassing goats in Absaroka Mountains.

c

13

# Bringing Back the Buffalo

High atop a wind-swept butte on the Moiese Refuge in western Montana, a number of visitors watched a wildlife spectacle that few have seen until recent years. Below them, late evening sun transformed stalks of summer-dried wheat grass to a soft rose-colored glow.

There, two giant bull buffalo backed ponderously away from one another until they stood no more than 20 feet apart. The mammoth beasts pawed angrily at the parched grass kicking dust high into the air.

Muscles tensed; then the animals bore down on one another colliding with such momentum that the sound of their impact carried far above the gusting wind of the sprawling plains. Again and again they repeated the ritual, colliding like locomotives, until it appeared as though the skull of each contestant would be shattered.

This brutal punishment continued for 15 to 20 minutes. Finally, just as the sun dipped into the towering peaks of a mountain range, one combatant turned groggily and staggered off. Too stunned to claim his prize of nearby cows, the victor stared glassily into space.

Montana has been the home for some of nature's most inspiring and most depressing dramas. Roll back the pages of history a few brief years and we see that the bison's story epitomizes both qualities. So numerous were the animals that hunters in the 1860s reported they lost sleep when unseen herds made the ground rumble and shake. Other westbound travelers of the same period reported herds they could not see across, while still others said buffalo blackened the plains not like cattle but like ants! But in five short years virtually every wild buffalo had been exterminated from the plains of North America, "their bones littering the prairie for mile after endless mile."

Many pages later another chapter has been written in the saga of the buffalo. The setting is different, but along the course of a 19-mile-long dirt road, we can still find bison dripping with water after charging through Pauline Creek or frothing with sweat following a brutal encounter on Antelope Ridge. But none of today's spectacles would have been possible had it not been for good fortune, good management and the intervention of an aroused public. Because of their acts there is a rekindled interest in bison. In response to this interest the National Bison Range opened its doors in the summer of 1982 to a $750,000 visitor center which further commemorates this animal. Through mural-sized photographs, slide presentations and displays, the history of the bison, the significant events that have occurred on the Range since its inception, and the part the National Bison Range played in recreating a genetically viable herd are re-enacted.

a

b

(a, b, c, d) Bison are rounded up each year and brought to corrals where they are identified for age and sex, inoculated against diseases and branded. Enough are culled from the herd to insure that those remaining will have adequate forage and be compatible with the carrying capacity of the range.

d

c

a

b

(a) The story of the West almost can be read in this bison's powerful visage.
(b) Michael Pablo had special wagons built to haul buffalo purchased for the Moiese reserve to a railhead. Pablo is shown leading a few of his buffalo wagons in this photo from the Elrod Collection, University of Montana Archives.

Conservation of the buffalo was not foremost in the minds of the first white settlers who dominated the area. Elimination of the bison as a source of sustenance for "recalcitrant Indians" was considered necessary to bring peace to the frontier.

Once the effort was underway, it took only a few short years to eliminate the buffalo from the plains. Congress subsequently responded by attempting to preserve a few remnants in Yellowstone National Park. One problem was poaching and, in 1893, 116 buffalo were killed illegally, reducing the park's herd to a mere handful. The following year, Congress enacted a law forbidding the shooting of buffalo under penalty of a thousand-dollar fine. This was the first strong action ever taken to insure the survival of the buffalo.

In 1905, conservation, of the buffalo acquired additional momentum by the formation of the American Bison Society. Theodore Roosevelt was elected honor-ary president, while William Hornaday served as the Society's active president. From then on it was a battle all the way, and the Society stopped at nothing to generate public awareness.

One prominent member, Ernest Harold Baynes, attempted to demonstrate the usefulness of bison to the general public by hitching-up a pair of four-month-old calves and putting them to the plow.

The superiority of his animals was demonstrated in a half-mile challenge race against experienced steers. The young buffalo won a decisive victory over their competitors, but here their story as domesticated beasts of burden ends. As the young bison matured, their strength and size made them impossible to handle.

Another effort to elicit public support was made by shearing young buffalo like so many sheep for their wool. This activity was aborted immediately; no amount of coddling could transform the pugnacious temperament of buffalo into that of docile sheep.

Financial and political difficulties also plagued the group, but strong lobbying action eventually paid off, and, in 1907, Congress finally appropriated funds necessary to stock the National Bison Range.

Bison that inhabit today's range have a unique origin. They date back to the spring of 1873 when Walking Coyote, a Pend d'Oreille Indian, was fortunate enough to capture four little buffalo calves, two bulls and two cows.

Coyote, together with his squaw and step-son, had been wintering with the Piegan Indians on the Milk River close to where Buffalo Lake now reposes. During a hunting expedition of which Coyote was a member, the four calves were cut out of a great herd. Strangely,

*Weigh-in at one of the first Bison Range roundups. One-ton buffalo were not nearly as cooperative as farm stock. In this photo from the Elrod Collection, a buffalo makes a last fierce struggle for freedom.*

young buffalo would follow hunters who had either slain their mothers or otherwise separated them.

Next spring, Walking Coyote took his four proteges to St. Ignatius Mission, the center of the Flathead Reservation. By then, they were unusually tame and soon became favored pets around the Mission.

When the two heifers were four years old, each had a calf and their numbers increased slowly year by year, until in 1884, they numbered 30 head. But their Indian owner, finding them too great a tax on his resources, decided to sell them. C. A. Allard, who was ranching on the reservation, was impressed with the possibility of a profitable investment in this small herd. A shrewd business man, he was quick to grasp an opportunity; he realized that within a few years the buffalo would be invaluable specimens. He successfully interested his friend and fellow rancher Michael Pablo in this project. The partners bought 10 of Walk-

ing Coyote's herd of 13 buffalo, paying $250 per head. This fortunate circumstance helped save the buffalo from extinction, for the herd grew until it became one of the largest in the world.

The fate of Walking Coyote was not as celebrated. After receiving his pay for the herd, he went to Missoula where he died several days later under one of the city's bridges from an overdose of alcohol — an ignominious end for the founder of today's National Bison Range herd.

Pablo and Allard retained the animals until the late 1890s, purchasing additional bison to infuse new blood into the herd. Then they sold the herd, part going to the Canadian Government and part to the Conrad Estate in Kalispell, Montana. From this herd the American Bison Society bought 34 animals. These bison, together with seven donated from other areas of the country, started the National Bison Range herd. On October 17, 1909, they were released, and the range, acquired on May of 1908 from the Flathead Indians, became a working refuge.

For many years after the establishment of the bison range, public visitation consisted mostly of locals. But in 1933, an albino bison was born to a brown cow. So unusual is an albino buffalo that Indians used to say "A white buffalo is so rare that even the Great Spirit is surprised to see one."

The effect of the white buffalo on the Great Spirit has not been recorded, but the birth of "Big Medicine" served to attract people from every state and many foreign countries. Montanans were proud of their white buffalo and thousands of school children were taken to see the lord of the range.

In the truest sense of the word, Big Medicine was not an albino, for he sported on his head tufts of brown hair. Still, he was a magnificent specimen. In his prime, Big Medicine weighed 1,900 pounds and measured six feet at the hump and close to 12 feet long from the tip of his nose to the end of his tail.

When Big Medicine reached 20 years, his health began to fail. First his hearing went, then it was discovered he was going blind from cancer of the eyes. His teeth were worn to the gums, necessitating that he be fed third cuttings of alfalfa, steamed barley soaked in molasses and special, high-protein rabbit pellets for the last year of his life.

Big Medicine died on the range where so many people had seen him. Immediately following his passing, radio stations in the area interrupted regular programming. The date was August 25, 1959.

Then director of the Montana Historical Society, the well known historian K. Ross Toole had arranged that

Big Medicine would remain on display in the Society's museum in Helena. The hide was tanned by a Colorado firm and nationally renowned taxidermist Bob Scriver was commissioned to make the full-life mount of Big Medicine.

Scriver remembers the event. On August 28, he drove to Moiese to pick up the carcass to be used as a model. "The animal smelled so bad," recalls Bob, "that I had to put a clothes pin on my nose to salvage him. Maggots were several inches thick, but we were able to salvage most of him."

When the tanned hide was returned to Browning, Scriver recalls that it had lost a lot of hair. He contacted the range personnel and requested brown hair from other buffalo. This hair was sent to Hollywood where it could be bleached to match Big Medicine, and Scriver attached the dyed hairs to the bare spots.

Though white bison are a one-in-60-million event, reports from the 1930s trickled in from Alaska that a white buffalo was part of an Alaskan herd. Perhaps these reports were based more on optimism than reality; in 1929, 23 buffalo from the Moiese herd had been shipped to Alaska. This group formed the nucleus of that state's present Big Delta herd. It was believed that the albino gene from the Moiese herd went north with those transplants. Numerous white calves have been born in that wild herd but, because they are deaf and blind, they do not survive long in the wild.

Today, bison and the bison range are doing exceedingly well. Some 300 to 400 bison roam within the confines of the 18,540-acre refuge. Sharing their domain are elk, bighorn sheep, mule and white-tailed deer and antelope.

Bison increase rapidly, and to maintain the population within the carrying capacity of the range, there is an annual roundup, which serves to cull out the surplus animals. The three-day-long roundup occurs the first week in October, and each year the event attracts thousands of spectators. (See "Bringing in the Buffalo" in the September, 1979 issue of MONTANA MAGAZINE.) They come to listen to the thunder of hooves flying across the sprawling plains. It is one of the refuge's many exciting stories summarized at the visitor center.

So thanks to Walking Coyote, Pablo and Allard, and an aroused public, America's great buffalo heritage need not be a mere abstraction in a Remington, Russell or Bodmer painting. For today on the National Bison Range, the progeny of the once mammoth herd that stretched from Canada to Mexico still churns waters brown, thunders into rose-hued sunsets, and violently enacts ancient rituals.

# ECOLOGY

Many of the significant improvements in management techniques have come about largely because of an increased understanding of ecology, the science that deals with the interrelationships of wildlife with their environment. Over the past four decades the idea of animals and plants dependent on one another to survive has become increasingly clear. This complex and dynamic interplay of living organisms is often called the web of life. Like a spider web, no strand can be pulled or loosened without affecting the whole web.

This "balance of nature" is anything but constant. Volcanic eruptions, floods, fires, earthquakes, insect epidemics and diseases all change the plant communities and so the animal populations. Man is also an agent of change. Farming, logging, mining, road building, dam construction, grazing, drainage projects, channelizations, range improvement projects, suburban sprawl and almost all other activities of man affect this delicate balance.

The plants and animals that exist on any particular site reflect this interdependence. Their existence can be predicted by factors such as elevation, depth and

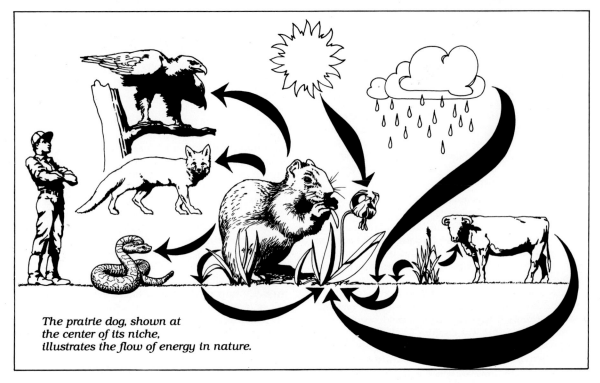

*The prairie dog, shown at the center of its niche, illustrates the flow of energy in nature.*

*Leopard frog with Monarch butterfly.*

type of soil, aspect and degree of slope, climate and precipitation, and wind patterns. Each organism has specific requirements and will grow or occur only where all those requirements are met.

Montana's vegetation, for instance, varies dramatically and reflects these specific requirements. Travelers moving from east to west across the state first encounter expansive prairies. The grasslands are dotted with shrubby hillsides, and coulees divided by cottonwood-guarded streams, and punctuated by rough breaks. In the central part of the state, isolated mountain ranges protrude above the prairies and support a variety of trees and shrubs. The almost continuous mountain ranges in the western part of the state receive more moisture than the rest of the state and are covered with lush forests, reminiscent of maritime climes.

To delineate the environs of the world, ecologists have divided them into broad groupings of similar vegetative types called biomes. Montana includes three such biomes, the grasslands, the taiga or coniferous forests, and the tundra. These broad vegetative regions are key factors in delimiting the abundance and distribution of animal species in the state.

a

b

c

d

(b) Grassland habitat near Malta, and its inhabitants. Shown here, (a) mule deer, (c) rabbit and (d) bittern.

# GRASSLANDS

The largest biome is the grasslands covering the eastern two-thirds of the state, it consists of a thick growth of annual and perennial plants, particularly grasses.

Here, the climate is extreme, characterized by sleet, hail and howling winds which desiccate the soil. Still, animals and plants that live here are in perfect harmony with their environment.

Many of the small mammals — prairie dogs, ground squirrels, pocket gophers, mice and badgers — take shelter in burrows in the cool earth. Larger mammals such as the coyote, mule deer, pronghorn and bison have thick coats that allow them to withstand the elements.

A variety of birds inhabits the grasslands. Undisturbed grasslands shelter birds such as the sharp-tailed grouse, bobolink, long-billed curlew and the western meadowlark. Ponds and marshes provide habitat for waterfowl, herons, shorebirds, gulls, terns and a number of water-loving songbirds. Agricultural areas, rocky breaks and river bottoms also have their corresponding complement of feathered inhabitants.

a

b

*(b) Taiga as seen along the east slope of the Rocky Mountains near Glacier. A fearsome hunter of the Taiga, the red tailed hawk (a).*

# TAIGA

The Russian word *taiga* is used to describe the wide coniferous forests that blanket much of the western third of the state. Within this region, the lower, drier sites are inhabited by ponderosa pine and Douglas fir interspersed with birch and aspen. Western red cedar, grand fir, western hemlock, western larch, Englemann spruce, western white pine and lodgepole pine, along with an occasional birch, grow on the moist slopes of the middle elevations. Ideal conditions for mountain hemlock, subalpine fir, and whitebark pine are found only at the higher elevations.

A host of small mammals are at home in the taiga. Mice, voles, chipmunks, tree squirrels, flying squirrels, beaver, porcupine, rabbits, weasels, mink and marten are some that can be found here. Among the large mammals of the area are the moose, elk, deer, grizzly bear, black bear, lynx, cougar and wolverine.

The forests provide shelter for an even greater variety of birds ranging from hummingbirds to hawks, turkeys to tanagers and from warblers to woodpeckers. The waters within the taiga provide food for the bald eagle, osprey, harlequin duck, red-breasted merganser, kingfisher and dipper.

Without a doubt, the largest variety of species and the greatest numbers of animals are found in the taiga biome.

a

b

*(a) Ptarmigan are year-round residents of the tundra. (b) Glacier Park has excellent examples of tundra ecology.*

# TUNDRA

Like islands in the sky, fragments of a third biome, the tundra, can be found on mountain tops across the state. The word tundra is also of Russian derivation. Although it refers to the treeless zone north of timberline found at the Arctic Circle, the terms also is applied to similar areas above timberline on high mountain peaks.

Tundra vegetation is low growing, adapted to the cold, is primarily perennial and consists mainly of grasses, mosses, lichens, sedges and shrubs. Stunted trees, twisted into grotesque forms by the gale winds and heavy snows, mark the lower edge of this biome.

Relatively few animals can survive in the harshest of Montana's habitats. Montana's champion hibernator, the hoary marmot can be found here along with the pika, Columbian ground squirrel, alpine chipmunk and ermine. Although many large mammals of the taiga move up the slopes to spend their summers on the alpine tundra, the mountain goat is the only large mammal capable of coping with the fierce winter weather.

As with the mammals, only a small number of birds inhabit the tundra. Rosy finches, water pipets, robins and a variety of other birds nest and/or feed on the low vegetation of this region. The largest of these birds and the only one that lives here all year, is the white-tailed ptarmigan.

# PHOTOSYNTHESIS

Animals are tied closely to vegetation in each biome because plants form a fundamental source of energy. Plants are unique in their ability to convert sunlight into forms of energy that can be used by animals. This process is referred to as photosynthesis and is one which utilizes carbon dioxide, water and the chlorophyll found within green plants. Because of this ability to convert sunlight into useable energy, plants are called producers.

# BIOLOGICAL PYRAMID

Plants form the base of what ecologists refer to as a biological pyramid. The pyramid illustrates the vast amount of energy that is lost as the food chain progresses from one level in the pyramid to the next higher level. Each time energy is converted from one form to another, energy is lost. Consequently, those animals near the top are larger, fewer in numbers and require far greater amounts of total energy to sustain them. Ecologists also believe the pyramid serves to illustrate the importance each life form plays in sustaining a viable wholeness. Remove a single life form from any of the levels and the total energy available to a higher level is diminished.

The next layer on the pyramid is made up of the primary consumers or those animals that eat vegetation and convert the stored energy into animal matter. They come in the shape of invertebrates, insects, fish, reptiles, amphibians, birds or mammals. They may eat the seeds, fruits, nuts, blossoms, leaves or stems of the plants.

Higher yet on the biological pyramid are the secondary consumers or those that feed on primary consumers. Again, they may belong to any of the various classes of animals.

Opportunists are animals that can function as either primary or secondary consumers — they can eat either plant or animal food. Examples are the grizzly bear, the coyote and the black bear.

*a*

*b*

(a) *Every form of life on earth is dependent on the process of photosynthesis which sustains this buttercup. Animals whose diet is based on plant life are primary consumers. (b) The coyote and magpie, both secondary consumers, feed on the carcass of an elk, a primary consumer.*

# NICHE

Within its broad function as a primary consumer or secondary consumers, each species has its own set of environmental requirements and its own set of activities that enable it to survive and make its living. Each species, then, has its own ecological niche, composed of a particular habitat and a particular means of feeding and surviving in that habitat. More than a physical space, a niche is a way of life, believed to be unique for each species. Although species may be similar, they usually are separated either spatially, temporally or behaviorally.

For example, the upland game birds are all large, ground dwelling birds that have similar means of feeding and surviving, they all eat seeds, insects and/or herbaceous material. But, they are spatially separated by their habitat requirements. In eastern Montana, the sharp-tailed grouse fills its niche in the grasslands while the sage grouse does the same in the sagebrush communities. Within the coniferous forests of western Montana, the blue grouse, ruffed grouse and the spruce grouse all seek out habitats dominated by differing species of trees.

The birds of prey demonstrate all three types of ecological separation. The American kestrel feeds primarily on insects, the osprey on fish, the peregrine falcon on birds and the great horned owl on mammals. Some, such as the golden eagle, hunt the open areas while others, such as the sharp-shinned hawk, hunt the woodlands. The eagles, hawks and falcons hunt by day or at dusk while most owls hunt at night.

# OBSERVING AND PHOTOGRAPHING WILDLIFE

a

I resembled a small haystack. A confused coyote was charging directly at me as though I were a free meal. I had not planned to be a main course, but then part of the fun of wildlife photography is in the unexpected.

Lured to the blind by a predator call that imitated the sound of a rabbit in distress, the coyote was too close to photograph and was still coming!

At six feet, I yelled. The coyote vaulted vertically into space as if each leg had been spring loaded. Needless to say, I didn't get a shot of this particular coyote; but at another stand, I scored.

In years past, both authors have shared their outdoor experiences through slide shows and invariably the vast majority of the questions asked pertained to camera makes and models. Apparently, the assumption is that the make, model and type of lens used determines the quality of picture that will be obtained. Nothing could be further from the truth!

While a good camera and lens is necessary for good photos, they do not guarantee satisfactory results. Good wildlife photos are taken by photographers that know their subjects and how to position themselves for best results. The very best photographers begin by observing their subjects. Only after becoming thoroughly familiar with the idiosyncrasies of the animal do they begin to photograph.

The first step to a photograph is locating a subject. A good place to begin looking is your own backyard. Appropriate plantings may already be attracting a variety of birds and animals to your yard. If not, numerous books and popular articles have been written on the subject of attracting birds and mammals. Well placed bird houses, bird baths or bird feeders will provide many hours of interesting observation. If placed with photography in mind, these structures can result in excellent photographs, perhaps taken from the comfort of your easy chair.

Other nearby places to observe and photograph wildlife are city and county parks. Squirrels, chipmunks, birds and ducks often are accustomed to being fed and become very tame. Taking advantage of these opportunities will improve your observation and photographic skills, increasing enjoyment when venturing into more remote or exotic areas.

Some of the best places to observe wildlife are the state and national wildlife refuges, parks and forests. While moving through these areas, keep your binoculars or camera close at hand. Even in these areas, where the animals may be accustomed to people, they may not stick around long enough for you to dig to the bottom of your suitcase to locate your binocs or camera. Wherever you decide to go, go either early or late in the day. Most wild creatures are more active and much more visible at these times. There is

*(a) Excellent areas to photograph birds may be found at wildlife refuges, such as Bowdoin Refuge near Malta.*
*(b) Virtually anything that breaks up the appearance of the human form will enable a photographer to approach the subject. For really shy species, blinds should be left standing to permit animals to acclimate to the object.*

b

no need to get really close to most animals to observe them. It is often more interesting, to watch from a distance while the animal goes about its business undisturbed. However, to get decent pictures, you will need to get close. Even with telephoto lenses, you will need to get much closer than you might think to get frame-filling shots of small or medium animals.

With the exception of those animals that have become so tame that your main problem is getting them far enough away to be able to focus, it takes knowledge, time and patience to get in close on wild animals. One method is the one I used to photograph the coyote — a blind. A hide, which is the European term, can be almost anything that screens you from the prying eyes of your quarry. In some areas, even wild animals have become accustomed to automobiles, enabling you to use your car as an effective blind. After locating a subject from a distance, pre-focus as accurately as possible, take a light reading and set your shutter speed and f-stop. Then proceed slowly toward the animal until you are close enough for a shot, turn off the engine, (the vibration of the running engine may ruin the picture, especially at slow shutter speeds), coast to a stop, fine focus and shoot. If the animal sticks around and you want to get closer, you can try restarting the engine, although this quite often ends the photo session. So, plan ahead to avoid moving once you have stopped.

Most other types of blinds are stationary and require some scouting and other preparation before the day of the foray to locate the right spot. Depending on the purpose and frequency of use, the blind may be built with vegetation cut from the surrounding area. Or, it may consist of a screen of artificial netting or a refrigerator shipping crate with appropriate lens ports and windows. More elaborate blinds may be custom made, or modified from pup-tents or ice houses. Permanent blinds constructed of wood to last for years are for the ambitious. When possible, a blind should be in place for several days to allow the animals time to accept it. However, I have set up blinds, crawled inside and begun shooting immediately. The success of this technique depends on the thoroughness of your scouting and on the temperament of the individual animal you are working with.

Even without blinds, animals often can be approached by following a few simple rules. First, because their senses are much sharper than ours, attempts at "sneaking up" on them usually fail. Their survival depends on them using their senses to the limit and that is what they do. Even if you do succeed in stalking close enough for a photo without them spotting you, the click of the shutter will alert them to

a

b

a

b

c

*Opposite Page:*

*(a) Even mechanical contraptions like strobes will be accepted by animals in time.*

*(b) Overlooking Lake Ellen Wilson in Glacier Park.*

*This Page:*

*(a) Approaching an animal diagonally rather than head-on often enables photographers to move close to their subjects.*

*(b) Photographer's dilemma.*

*(c) Backpackers stop to admire goat at Gunsight Pass, Glacier National Park.*

your presence and that is usually the end of the session.

A much more successful method is to approach the animal openly, making no attempt to hide. Instead, every attempt should be made to allow the animals to see you at a distance. The approach is then made slowly and indirectly. Approach the animal at an angle, stopping at the first sign of nervousness on the part of the animal. When the animal has calmed down and resumed his normal activities, continue the approach, even more slowly, in the general direction of the animal.

During this type of approach, a couple of things are of paramount importance. The first is not to make any sudden moves or noises because, in the animal's world, sudden moves are usually indicative of predators. Consequently, most animals will flee, even if there is no real danger. The other thing is to appear nonchalant and try not to look directly at the animal. Many animals, particularly the larger mammals, equate a direct stare with a predator gauging the distance for the attack and will spook. Eye contact in particular should be avoided.

A couple of final tips: Practice with your camera on more familiar subjects to gain ease in obtaining correct exposures, and to quickly obtain accurate focusing and good composition. The practice will pay off with good photos instead of excuses when the chance of a lifetime presents itself and disappears, all within an instant.

Spend as much time looking over your pictures when they come back from the developer as you did while taking them. While it is good to read books and talk to experienced photographers, the real learning comes from doing and analyzing the results. Figure out what could have been done to improve the picture.

Probably the biggest mistake beginners make when taking wildlife photos is not getting close enough. For a portrait, the animal should at least fill the larger circle visible in the view finder or about one-third of the frame. Many photographers believe the animal should fill at least one-half the frame.

When the opportunity presents itself to take pictures, take advantage of it — don't wait until tomorrow. Innumerable photo opportunities have been missed because the photographer broke this rule. Birds fledge, desert their nests, get killed by predators, find new food sources and migrate. Mammals alter their habits, move their dens, search for greener pastures or get killed. The weather turns bad, leaves drop and the flowers are eaten or stop blooming. Many things can happen and good intentions do not show on the screen.

# MAMMALS

Mammals have certain characteristics that distinguish them from other animal groups. They are warm-blooded animals, maintaining a fairly constant body temperature. They have a four-chambered heart and a highly developed nervous system. The body is more or less covered with hair. The female has glands for nourishing the young with milk.

The following groups of mammals are found in Montana and the common representatives of each group have been described in this book.

## 1. INSECT-EATING MAMMALS.
(Order Insectivora)
Description: A group of small primitive animals with a long, pointed nose, and feet adapted for burrowing undrground.
Examples: moles, shrews.

## 2. WINGED MAMMALS.
(Order Chiroptera)
Description: Mammals that have wings and other specialized structures for true flight.
Examples: Bats are the only flying mammals.

## 3. RABBIT-LIKE MAMMALS.
(Order Lagomorpha)
Description: Structurally similar to the rodents, though with several features recognized by mammologists. One variation is their dentition (teeth); members of this order have four upper incisors instead of a single pair.
Examples: hares, rabbits, pika.

## 4. GNAWING MAMMALS.
(Order Rodentia)
Description: Teeth adapted for gnawing; have chisel-like pair of incisors that continue growth throughout life of the animal as the surface is worn away; back of the incisors are the molars for grinding. Largest single order of mammals, in number of species and individuals.
Examples: mice, pocket gophers, rats, squirrels, ground squirrels, chipmunks, woodchucks, prairie dog, beaver, muskrat, porcupine.

## 5. FLESH-EATING MAMMALS.
(Order Carnivora)
Description: Adapted for living mainly on flesh by having small incisor teeth and large, projecting canine teeth for cutting and tearing flesh. Most animals of the group have a keen sense of smell enabling them to follow their prey.
Examples: mountain lion, Canada lynx, bobcat, wolf, coyote, foxes, weasels, mink, black-footed ferret, marten, fisher, wolverine, otter, skunk, badger, raccoon, bears.

## 6. EVEN-HOOFED MAMMALS.
(Order Artiodactyla)
Description: Support their bodies on the third and fourth toes; other toes have been reduced in size or lost. Have strong molar teeth with broad surfaces for grinding the plant food on which they live.
Examples: elk, deer, bison, pronghorn, sheep.

# INSECT-EATING MAMMALS

Although shrews are among our most abundant mammals they are seldom seen or recognized by most people. They are mouse-shaped animals with long, slender noses, tiny eyes, and ears hidden in the soft fur. Shrews are often mistaken for mice or moles, the latter of which do not occur in the state. Since they do not hibernate, shrews leave their tunnels in the snow as they search for food under fallen leaves and grasses.

Shrews are classed as insect-eaters, but the larger species will eat the flesh of any small animal that they can kill. Mice and small birds may fall prey to these fearless little hunters. A two-ounce mouse, for example, is no match for the fury of a half-ounce shrew.

The secret of a shrew's success as a predator is a gland in its mouth which contains a potent nerve poison similar to that of some venomous snakes. The poison flows with the shrew's saliva into the body of a bitten victim. A mouse bitten by a shrew will die in several minutes; a human will experience discomfort.

Just as shrews are quick to devour mice, insects and worms — any animal within their capability — so other predators may pounce on them. Thus their occupation or niche is that of both prey and predator. Hawks, snakes, weasels and foxes feed on them and frequently their bones are found in pellets regurgitated by owls.

Shrews are among the most primitive of mammals and remains of their teeth have been found on the Charles M. Russell National Refuge interspersed with the bones of dinosaurs. Seventy million years ago they were coinhabitants, but where one flourished, the other eventually perished.

Today, 27 varieties of shrews inhabit North America, from arctic tundra to arid sagebrush plains and from lowland bogs to timberline. Shrews in Montana include the masked, Hayden, vagrant, Merriam, dwarf, water, Prebel and pygmy.

The shrew would be amazing for its size alone. The pygmy shrew weighs only a fraction of an ounce and is probably the smallest living mammal.

Another shrew that has made an interesting adaptation to its environment is the water shrew. It lives near streams lush with vegetation where it is occasionally seen scampering along the surface of the water. Little pockets of air, trapped by stiff hairs that fringe its feet, enable the water shrew to perform this amazing feat.

*The ability to fly is just one of the bat's bizarre adaptations. Shown here a Western big-eared bat.*

# FLYING MAMMALS

Perhaps the most maligned and misunderstood mammals in Montana are the bats. Rarely do they deserve the sinister reputations associated with them in passages from an Edgar Allen Poe story or scenes from a Vincent Price movie. More appropriately, bats might deserve a place in Ripley's *Believe it or Not.*

Bats are the only mammals that can fly. (The flying squirrel can only glide in an ever descending line from its point of origin.) Unlike most birds, which fly with the bones of their "arms" and attached feathers, bats fly with their "fingers" and the skin that spans these digits. Like birds, bats achieve flight by closing their wings and extending them on the down beat. In this manner, bats are very agile and can twist, turn, and dodge with the same degree of dexterity of most birds. Bats may even drink while in full flight.

Since most of a bat's activities occur at night, it might be logical — if it weren't for the "blind as a bat" cliche — to assume that these creatures have evolved exceptional night-time vision. Bats are not blind, but neither do they have exceptional sight.

Bats navigate by issuing a steady stream of high-pitched sounds from their voice boxes. These sounds range in frequency from 30,000 cycles — or the upper limit of human hearing — to 60,000 cycles or higher per minute. If a bat picks up a echo from one of its sounds, it increases the rate of discharge until the signals are going and coming at a rate of 50-60 per second. These sounds provide bats much information: Is the object returning the echo an obstacle, or is it something to eat? If the latter, in which direction is the morsel moving? In this manner, bats can locate their prey or navigate through a maze of obstacles such as a series of closely strung wires.

Bats as a group eat a great variety of food to include frogs, mice, small birds and insects. They have huge appetites and each will eat more than half its weight every night. Bats need this enormous intake of food for they expend a great deal of energy, the replacement of which depends not only on an ample supply of food, but also on the high metabolic rate with which they are blessed. Associated with these characteristics is a heart that pulses at a speed of 700 beats per minute — higher than that of any other mammalian species.

Most animals that lead fast-paced lives die at a relatively early age. Bats are the exception, with some species living 20 years or more. Perhaps their longevity is due to a deep winter sleep — a breather so to speak — which some bats must undergo to escape the harshness of winter. In Montana, the big-eared bat moves deep within caves found throughout the state, while the long-eared myotis escapes the winter by flying south.

Just prior to hibernation, bats mate. Embryos develop very slowly or may even remain suspended. This occurs while sleeping and food intake is nonexistent. Such a condition of embryonic cessation is referred to as delayed implantation and results when the fertilized egg does not become attached to the placenta. Several months later when the eggs does become attached, the embryo begins to develop.

Shortly after hibernation, female bats retire to "maternity wards" where they give birth to blind and naked young. One such ward can be seen at the Lewis and Clark Caverns where about 200 big-eared bats congregate each year.

The world contains more than 2,000 species of bats, and North America claims at least 250. Of these Montana has 12. Each occupies a unique ecological niche which reduces competition among the various species for common resources.

Throughout the United States, bat populations have declined in recent years. Primary causes are widespread use of DDT and disturbance of roosts by cave explorers. In Montana, however, bat species are thought to be secure.

# RABBIT-LIKE MAMMALS

The bounding white-tailed jack rabbit that inhabits virtually all but the extreme northwestern portion of Montana is actually a hare, not a rabbit. (Three types of hares and four types of rabbits live in Montana.)

Hares differ from rabbits in many respects, the most conspicuous being their longer ears and larger hind legs and feet in relation to their body size. Hares (jackrabbits) are also born with full ears, functional eyes and have a capability for hopping around within hours

28

a

c

b

*a*

*b*

*c*

*Opposite Page: (a & b) Protective camouflage is a survival adaptation that enables many small mammals to evade their predators. In winter, most hares are as white as fresh-fallen snow. (c) White-tailed rabbit in summer coat.*

*Above: (a) Snowshoe hare.*

*(b) Cottontail along Missouri River.*

*(c) Mountain cottontail.*

after birth. Rabbits are born naked and completely helpless.

Scientists further separate lagomorphs, or any member of the rabbit family, from rodents with which they are occasionally grouped by amateurs. Lagomorphs have a small pair of incisors immediately behind the large pair of upper ones. Rodents do not.

Rabbit-like mammals have a remarkable means of obtaining the maximum value from their food. Their fecal material is of two types: moist pellets with residual food value and dry pellets, the products of which are wastes. Moist pellets are expelled and later eaten by swallowing without chewing. Thus, the food, which usually consists of grasses and other herbaceous plants, travels through the digestive tract twice.

Populations of both rabbits and hares are subject to great fluctuations, and their presence or absence affects the ecological balances in areas in Montana. Some predators, such as bobcats, lynx, hawks and owls, increase with any proliferation of these animals. Then following a "bust" or decline in the number of lagomorphs, these animals may all but disappear.

Rabbits and hares avoid their enemies by taking full advantage of their physical characteristics. Helping them avert disaster are a sensitive nose and ears so perceptive that they can detect the muted sound of a coyote as its fur brushes lightly against the grass. Eyes set far back on their heads also help these animals perceive danger whether it comes from in front, above, to the side, or even behind. After evaluating the situation, hares and rabbits may freeze in place and make their bodies blend with their surroundings.

If camouflage fails, they can rely on their tremendous physical prowess. Hares are endowed with powerful hind legs and, if flushed, often escape with marathon sprints and leaps. They have been measured running at speeds up to 35 miles per hour, vaulting six feet high and leaping distances of 20 feet.

Courtship ceremonies of hares and rabbits are wild affairs. Bucks, as male hares are called, may stand on the toes of their hind feet and box each other furiously with their front feet. Usually there is no sound other than the thud-thud-thud of rapid-fire blows. Damage is often inflicted and should a jackrabbit be seen with torn ears or a gash along its side, it is safe to assume that damage was the result of male antagonism.

Hares and rabbits are both known for their fertility — "As prolific as a rabbit," goes the saying, which is not an exaggeration, particularly when speaking of Montana's cottontails. If all progeny survived from a single pair, they would number more than 300,000 at the end of a five-year period.

a

c

b

# PIKA

Few animals are rugged enough to live actively the entire year in a region where howling winds drive cold snows over their homes. Most mammals must either hibernate or migrate. But the pika does neither.

Densely furred, these small mammals are well prepared for life in the highest and harshest community in rock slides adjacent to alpine meadows. Of equal importance is the fact that the lean winter months do not catch these enterprising little creatures unprepared. During the summer, pikas may be seen hopping across rocks and scurrying out to a favorite plant. Using its sharp incisors, the pika clips off the stem, collects the plant in its mouth, and then dashes off to another one. Once a mouthful has been gathered, the pika finds a suitable rock and deposits its harvest on a steadily increasing pile for curing. Before summer's end, one five-ounce pika may have gathered as much as 30 pounds of grasses, sedges or herbs and distrib-

uted it like so many piles of hay. Following the short alpine summer, pikas live actively but snuggly, beneath rocks, subsisting during the winter on their miniature stacks of hay.

Pikas are common in Montana's mountain areas though the extension of their eastern range seems to end with the Big Snowy Mountains near Lewistown. These tailless Lagomorphs with diminutive ears are most abundant in subalpine and alpine habitats, but are also found in montane coniferous forests at lower elevations.

Little is known about the life history of pikas; inclement weather conditions make study too difficult. Biologists know they are preyed upon by hawks and weasels inhabiting the same area and that they protect themselves with the high-pitched "Ka-ack, Ka-ack" which often surprises timberline hikers venturing near talus slopes and boulder fields.

*(a) The pika is a tailless member of the rabbit family.*

*(b & c) Pikas do not hibernate. Rather, they gather vegetation into small "haystacks." The dried grasses serve as food during the long winter.*

# GNAWING MAMMALS

## GROUND SQUIRRELS

As you travel across the plains or hike through mountain meadows, you see them standing erect at the mouths of their burrows like tin soldiers. No wonder early day pioneers referred to them as "picket pins."

Dozens of other names also have been applied to Montana's six species of ground squirrels, the most common appelation being "gopher." The term, however, is a misnomer. True gophers are subterranean animals having small eyes, which are virtually functionless.

Ground squirrels, on the other hand spend a great deal of time above ground, though they seek sanctuary in an elaborate maze of underground tunnels.

For all the confusion, largely in telling one from the other, ground squirrels can be differentiated from their rodent cousins. They are smaller than marmots, and are altogether different from pocket gophers.

Ground squirrels, as a group, are small, slender animals with large eyes, small ears set low on their head, and have cheek pouches. These pouches have an enormous capability for transferring food from one location to another and naturalists have removed more than 200 seeds from their capacious pouches.

Color among the ground squirrels is varied and tends to blend with the patterns or hues of the country with which they are associated. Biologists refer to this camouflage exterior as "protective coloration."

All of the ground squirrels are burrowers. They construct complex underground networks, which many Montana farmers considered a curse.

Burrows typically have several entrances, with no tell-tale mounds showing. Excess dirt is carried away in their cheek pouches. At night, entrances are plugged with grasses or sod. Openings two-inches in diameter lead to a tunnel that may plummet four feet straight down. At that point, the tunnel turns abruptly and branches. Each of the various corridors serves a specific function. One may serve as a nest, while others may function as a storage chamber or as an escape hatch.

*a*

*d*

*(a) The golden-mantled ground squirrel's stripes cease at its neck.*

*(b) Ground squirrels (here a Columbian ground squirrel) stand erect when alarmed. Early settlers thus referred to them as "picket pins."*

*(c) Agricultural practices have altered the habitat of the once abundant 13-lined ground squirrel.*

*(d) Richardson's ground squirrel.*

*b*

*c*

31

a

b

Ground squirrels are preyed upon by virtually any animal considered to be a predator. Depending on the habitat and species indigenous to that area, ground squirrels may be preyed upon by coyotes, foxes, bears, skunks, minks, weasels, hawks, owls, snakes and badgers. The result is that they have evolved into highly alert and perceptive little mammals.

Though ground squirrels are usually solitary in nature, they tend to be colonial in the sense that they build burrows close to others of their kind. The association is beneficial. Listen to one chirp as it is approached. Others in the area freeze. If a second signal is given, they may be seen scurrying to the nearest burrow.

Time away from their burrows is spent gathering food. Scampering within a home range of about one acre they gather a variety of vegetable materials. One species, the thirteen-lined ground squirrel, has become carnivorous, including in his menu lizards, eggs, young birds and mice.

Ground squirrels are one of the state's true hibernators, and early fall finds them preparing chambers designed to protect them from freezing. Then, at the first sign of snow they curl up and sleep for as long as eight full months. Biologists at the Montana State University Veterinarian Lab, who have monitored hibernating ground squirrels in captivity tell us that body temperatures drop from a high of 106 degrees to 37 degrees Fahrenheit. Heartbeats may slow from a high of 350 beats per minute to five. Respiration rates drop from 50 breaths a minute to four. During this sleep these little animals can lose as much as one-third to one-half of their body weight.

Ground squirrels emerge from hibernation in mid-April, as a drive from Browning to Augusta on Highways 89 and 287 will quickly confirm. Snows still cover the ground, yet somehow, they find food and time to mate. Gestation is about 28 days so litters averaging eight to 10 begin to appear by mid-May. Young are born blind, toothless and weigh no more than a tenth of an ounce. For almost a month, they are completely helpless, but at the end of that time they are weaned and enough escape their myriad of enemies to propogate a generation or two their own.

*(a & b) Backpack raider — Hikers venturing into arctic-alpine habitats who leave packs unattended invite the invasion of ground squirrels which may chew sweaty straps for salt as well as deplete a backpacker's food supply.*

*(c) Flying squirrel*

c

# FLYING SQUIRREL

As you tromp through the woods each fall, you frequently come across a pile of pine-cone seeds at the base of a tree or along the bark of a rotting log. Many of the piles were left by the broad-toothed red squirrel. But not all. Examine the pile, and if you see fine tooth marks on the cones, it indicates the gnawer was one of the most common, but seldom seen, and one of the most intresting, but difficult to study small mammals inhabiting Montana.

Meet the northern flying squirrel, an animal that does not fly in the sense that bats do, but has been trying so hard for so long that it has become a topnotch glider.

Out on a far limb now, perhaps 100 feet above the ground, the squirrel bunches its feet together. Then, it leaps into space. Immediately it spreads its legs causing the membrane connecting its body and legs to stretch taut. The effect is to increase surface area providing the animal with "lift." So equipped, flying squirrels can control the speed and length of glide. Its angle of glide is directed by the tail, which also serves to position it for landing. A quick flip with this appendage and up snaps the head repositioning the body for the moment of impact. Then, like a parachute, the membrane slows the glide; padded feet help absorb the shock of landing.

a

b

# TREE SQUIRRELS

In addition to the flying squirrel, two species of tree squirrels inhabit Montana — the red and the fox. Smallest of the two is the red squirrel which is more often heard than seen. In fact, one will probably locate you first and then proceed to publicize both his presence and yours with a furor of harsh chatter. To find the noisy informant, stop for a moment, look overhead, and you may spot a tail-flickering motion. Attached to the tail is a small rusty body that may be confused with the chickaree, indigenous to more western states. If you are unable to locate the source of chatter, scan the ground for large piles of gnawed conifer cones, indicating which trees are regularly inhabited. Like other tree squirrels, the red does not hibernate. During the coldest days they remain in the warm nests in the crotches of branches or in hollow trees.

Relatively new to the state is the fox squirrel, largest of North America's tree squirrels. Still confined largely to the eastern part of the state, fox squirrels have been moving up the Missouri River and into the cottonwood forests along the valleys of the larger rivers since about 1940. This rusty colored species is yellowish-brown on the belly and grayish-brown above. Although nuts may be the preferred food, corn and other grains are often stored in hollow trees.

Fox and red squirrels are thought to sire two litters of young a year. Both species produce about three to four young that are born naked and blind. Predators are numerous and include hawks and owls. Red squirrels have the particular misfortune of having to contend with the pine marten.

c

Flying squirrels often pick old, hollowed-out snags in which to nest — just the kind we firewood gatherers like to harvest. In fact, one Montana study revealed that more than 40 such creatures once inhabited such a tree.

Flying squirrels are active year around. They mate twice a year, generally in March and then again in May through July. The young are born after a 40-day gestation period and the litter averages three to four in number. New born are naked and pink, have their eyes and ears closed, and weigh about one-ninth of an ounce. Males are not permitted to see their young and it is doubtful whether flying squirrel couples remain together other than during the mating season.

Flying squirrels are considered old at three and seldom live past the age of six; they have too many enemies: hawks, owls, raccoons, martens, weasels and bobcats all help to keep their numbers down. University studies indicate that a typical Douglas fir or spruce-fir forest averages about five or six of these mammals per acre. Though their distribution throughout Montana is not well known, it is known they are abundant in western Montana and that their range probably ends in the mountains of central Montana.

*(a) With a quick upward thrust of its tail, the flying squirrel reorients its body, slows its descent by spreading the parachute-like membrane connecting its legs and prepares to land.*

*(b) Nesting areas for the flying squirrel are located in old, hollowed snags.*

*(c) Three species of tree squirrels inhabit Montana. Shown here, the red squirrel.*

*(d) A flickering tail is a characteristic action of the red squirrel.*

d

33

# PRAIRIE DOGS

Prairie dogs are colonial rodents whose underground dwellings once stretched through the Great Plains from Texas to Montana. At one time their towns were hundreds of square miles in size with populations numbering in the hundreds of thousands.

Today, only a few colonies remain, preserved primarily by conservation agencies such as the U.S. Fish and Wildlife Department. Several of these towns stretch for several miles, though few exceed 400 to 500 acres. Areas outside these "islands" were reduced by ranchers around the turn of the century when they found they had to shoot a favorite horse or a valuable steer because it stepped into a prairie dog hole and broke its leg.

If given the chance, prairie dogs consume large amounts of forage. It has been said by range managers that 32 of them will consume enough forage to feed a sheep for a year and 256 will eat the 'keep' of a cow. Understandably, a war was waged against these "varmints." Weapons included poisoned grain, traps, strychnine gas and, of course, every caliber of firearm devised. Like the buffalo, they perished by the millions.

Despite the nuisance factor, prairie dogs are among the state's most interesting rodents. Two species occur, though one, the white-tailed prairie dog, barely reaches into south-central Montana. It is found along the Clark's Fork of the Yellowstone River where its habits vary in some ways from those of its close cousin. One significant characteristic is that white-tailed prairie dogs are deep winter sleepers. The other species, the black-tailed prairie dog, is the variety once so common east of the Continental Divide, and it is not a hibernator. Even on the coldest of winter days it may be seen gnawing on a piece of dried up grass.

Prairie dogs spend a considerable amount of time and effort on their dwellings, which are some of the most elaborate homes devised by any American mammal. Typically, burrows in a town go straight down two or three feet and then branch into a labyrinth of tunnels. Within the burrow, there are a variety of rooms. Invariably, there is a guard room or listening post. Here the prairie dog listens carefully before venturing outside. Other rooms consist of a bedroom, lined with mats of dried grass, and a toilet.

The crater-shaped mound surrounding the entrance may be as much as two feet high and four feet in diameter. This mound serves to protect the burrow from buffeting winds and keeps the chamber dry.

*a*

*b*

*c*

(a) Standing near a mound, a prairie dog assumes an alert stance. Should it sense danger, it will emit a series of barks that brings others in the community to attention.

(b) Grooming is a common practice among members of a "coterie."

(c) Prairie dogs chew down all vegetation that surrounds their mounds for a better view of predators.

Water, from summer cloud bursts, often stands several inches on the surface and the elevated mound prevents water from innundating the underlying labyrinth.

Mounds also serve as a watching post. At the slightest indication of danger a sentinel will emit a series of barks that bring others in the town to attention. A soaring bird need do no more than cast a shadow and prairie dogs begin voicing their concern.

Barking is contagious and spreads across the entire colony. Within moments there is an incessant din of chatter that swells in intensity. Dogs begin dashing for home and from the vantage of their elevated mounds the barking continues until the danger either passes or the prairie dogs are forced into the security of their burrows. Once the danger has passed, another signal is given. "Wee-oo, wee-oo," goes the refrain.

Prairie dog predators come in many forms. Once the black-footed ferret was a major threat. Today, it is an endangered species and is very rare. Still, prairire dogs respond as in days of old by plugging burrows they suspect are occupied by ferrets. A concentration of plugged burrows is an indicator these endangered animals may be occupying the area.

Other enemies include hawks, eagles, coyotes, foxes, and the notorious badger. Old "pick and shovel" is a formidable adversary particularly when prairie dogs have constructed a single entrance leading into their burrows. Then, there is no escape and an easy dinner for the badger is assured.

Prairie dog communities are a crossroad for other species of wildlife. Mountain plovers, toads, salamanders and a variety of prairie birds all seek the short-grass habitat occupied by prairie dogs. Once bison frequented these areas where they would roll in the dust.

Two other conspicuous adversaries are rattlesnakes and burrowing owls. When snakes appear, prairie dogs beat a hasty retreat, but burrowing owls and prairie dogs are more compatible. Burrowing owls don't eat prairie dogs, but they aggravate the occupants of the burrows to such an extent that they soon leave. Burrows then become the owl's place of residence where they carry on activities similar to those of prairie dogs. Before the arrival of white man and his chemical eradication programs, burrowing-owl populations were common in the state. Studies have shown that the poisoning of a prairie dog town simultaneously renders the burrows useless for burrowing owls.

Though scientists have observed prairie dogs for a long time, only superficial details are known about the most personal aspects of their lives.

Breeding occurs somewhere between March to May and evidently birth can take place from May on. Litter sizes average four in number and young are born blind and helpless. Eyes open 33 to 37 days after birth. Wearning occurs at about six weeks of age at which time they learn the lesson of territoriality from their neighbors. If a youngster strays into a neighbor's territory, a penetrating bite will send it scampering back to its own family unit.

Prairie dogs have an elaborate social organization known as a "coterie." This unit usually consists of a male, several females and their litter of pups. Within these coteries, or family units, there is apprently total harmony. Grooming, nursing, and play frequently take place. Each coterie also displays a strong tendency to defend its territory from intrusion by surrounding coteries.

Black-tail prairie dogs expand their towns by moving out and leaving the juveniles that are near adult size behind.

*A maze of mounds is evidence the pocket gopher has been active all winter.*

## POCKET GOPHERS

Members of this family are the only true American gophers. They have large fur-lined cheek pouches used for carrying, which open outside the mouth. Most of their feeding and other activities are carried on underground by an extensive series of tunnels. Piles of dirt on top of the ground show evidence of their presence.

During the winter pocket gophers continue to tunnel close to the surface where they leave a maze of conspicuous mounds of soil that may wind for hundreds of yards. It is estimated that the soil they inhabit is completely worked and turned every two years. Two species of pocket gophers inhabit Montana.

## MICE

Millions of miles of frequently used trails wind back and forth among the various life zones of Montana. These trails, though very small in size, are not only well defined but are easily detected by those so inclined. Along these trails travel most members of a furred group of rodents collectively called mice by the layman.

Biologists differentiate mice and further categorize them not only as mice but as lemmings and voles. Although even experts have trouble identifying them, the following will serve as a general guide to their characteristics.

Eight voles that vary in size from about four to ten inches long, including the tail, live in Montana. All are distinguished by their short hind legs, short furred tail, and ears that can just barely be seen.

Lemmings of more northern fame are represented by the Northern bog lemming. The bog lemming, as its name implies, makes its home in wet bogs and meadows where there is a thick mat of ground vegetation. If its shorter tail is not noticed, it easily can be confused with a vole.

*Montana's most abundant mammal, the deer mouse.*

*a*

*b*

*(a) Mice have no means of defense and rely on protective camouflage to elude predators.*
*(b) An assemblage of young voles. Note the lack of conspicuous ears which differentiates this species from other mouse-like animals.*

Mice, as most people know them, are represented in Montana by four species. They may be distinguished from other mouse-like animals by their large conspicuous eyes, ears, and long tails. Of the various Montana species, the one most likely to be seen outside is the deer mouse. Not only does it occupy most vegetative communities, but it is the most common mammal in the state. One interesting feature of the deer mouse is its homing instinct. Scientists have discovered that if captured and released it will find its way home — even from a distance of several miles.

*c*

a

b

c

d

e

*Opposite Page: (c) Beavers were the vital link in opening large sections of the West to civilization. Today, naturalists say their presence is "the key to wildlife abundance." (a) Probably no other animal can so alter the environment. (b) A busy beaver. (c) The warning splash. (d) Beaver workings along Nevada Creek and (e) the Sun River.*

# BEAVER

Without stretching the truth, it can be said that the beaver, the largest of all North American rodents, was as instrumental as any factor in opening up a large area west of the Mississippi to civilization. Seldom in the history of fabrics have the influences of fashion been so strong. But the fact is that a man wearing a beaver hat in the early 1800s was considered to be a real Dapper Dan. So great was the demand for beaver hides that industrial empires were founded on the traffic of skins brought back from the western frontier.

In the area that later became Montana, beaver and "made beaver" became the monetary system of the frontier. The impact of the beaver-pelt currency appeared in the Flathead-Salish Indian language when the word "ska-le-oo," originally meaning beaver, become the term for money. During that era, trade goods might be priced at five beaver for an axe, one beaver for a pound of gunpowder, one beaver for a knife, four beaver for a steel trap, one-fourth beaver for a string of beads and one beaver for a hand mirror.

Beaver stopped contributing to the world of fashion in the 1850s when the style of hats changed from fur to silk. By then inroads had been made into the West and the beaver was given a reprieve, once again free to exert its own natural influence.

Like all rodents, the beaver has two pair of gnawing teeth — one pair in the upper and another in the lower jaw. A space separates them from the chewing teeth which are located further back in the mouth. These large front teeth are one of the beaver's most distinguishing features and enable it to perform such feats as felling a tree more than a foot and half in diameter.

Other anatomical features allow beavers to thrive in water, while equally remarkable habits help them create and maintain conditions necessary for their survival. Their underfur — of an unusually soft, smooth and dense quality — traps air, insulating the beaver's skin from contact with water or cold air. The animal's legs are short and strong. The large hind feet have five webbed toes, forming a powerful paddle. The two inside toes have split claws with which the beaver grooms itself. The front feet are smaller and not webbed. The trademark of the beaver is its broad, flattened, scaly tail. Ten to twelve inches long and six inches wide, it is used for steering and, to a lesser extent, for propulsion when the animal swims. The tail also serves as a prop when a beaver stands while gnawing, or when it carries mud, stones, grass, or other

a

*(a) Beaver house and tracks in the snow along Nevada Creek. (b) Yellow-bellied marmot. (c) Marmot siblings.*

materials with the forefeet to plaster a lodge or a dam.

Many naturalists refer to the beaver as "the key to wildlife abundance." The story of this gnawer's impact on nature might logically begin with a young beaver that has just been harassed out of an over-populated colony. Leaving the safety of the water, the animal travels cross-country during the security of night, hiding during the day in thickets or brush. Eventually, the animal comes to a shallow stream flowing gently through a narrow valley in the mountains. Again, by the cover of night, the animal quickly begins to fashion a dam. Instinct guides the beaver in its work and hurries it on. The beaver knows that until the water rises it is vulnerable to mountain lions, bobcats, coyotes and a variety of hawks, owls and eagles.

Within a week a small dam is complete, but as time goes on and other beavers join to form a colony, the dam may enlarge. In areas of Montana, where beavers are abundant, many dams span a quarter of a mile; one measured 2,140 feet. Sometimes these dams are considered a nuisance and attempts are made to discourage beavers from further constructing them by pouring creosote on trees, brush and sticks, or directly on the dams. Many beaver dams have even been dynamited or bulldozed. But a particularly determined beaver fights back. Nothing, it seems, short of death is going to deter the animal from building its dam right where it wants. If traps are left, a set-wise beaver may spring the trap with a stick and then weave the trap into the dam.

If the dam is being constructed by a pair, together they improve upon the structure and then settle in to build a lodge. First brush is sunk into the bottom and weighted with rocks. Then, as construction pro-

gresses, several underwater entrances to the house are fashioned. When completed, the house projects three to five feet above the water and is an unimpregnable fortress. In their efforts to create a secure environment for themselves the pair has laid the groundwork for altering the landscape. Snug in their new surrounding, the pair nestles in to wait out the onslaught of winter.

In some areas of Montana such as the Missouri, where waters are deep and slow, beavers have modified their behavior. Here adequate protection exists in these deep-bodied rivers, and beavers have little reason to construct dams or lodges. In these areas, beavers burrow into the side of banks and excavate chambers. Logically, beavers inhabiting these areas are referred to as "bank beaver." Elaborate chambers constructed by bank beavers serve the same functions as the dams and lodges on Montana's other rivers and streams.

In late spring, the family increases in size. Four small, fully furred kits weighing about one pound apiece are born. At three weeks they take to the water and quickly learn the beaver's technique for swimming. Kicking with their hind feet and permitting the front feet to trail loosely along side their breasts, they glide, selecting their chosen course with the aid of their tails.

As the years pass the kits build lodges of their own — joined, perhaps, by others that have been expelled from saturated colonies. Together, they insure that the pond will grow.

b

Eventually, sediments are carried down by the stream to form a rich fertile muck. Pond weeds and lilies find their way in and begin to grow in wild profusion. Cover for dusk is now available and they soon begin to raise broods of their own. Toward the center, fish feed, attracting birds that can prey on fish. Not unpredicatably, anglers consider beaver ponds ideal areas for catching pan-sized fish.

In time, perhaps 50 years or more, the beavers' food sources of aspen, willow and cottonwood diminish, and they are forced to move to another area having an adequate supply of food. Eventually the old dam falls into a state of disrepair and gives way, leaving behind a broad expanse of fertile mud suitable for the germination of grasses and sedges. Soon the area is altered again, but now it becomes a broad meadow of grass that rolls in the mountain wind. Tiny voles thread trails through this lush vegetation and deer find cover and a plentiful supply of food.

Few creatures in our natural world have the capability to so alter the landscape in such a short period of time, as does the beaver.

c

# Marmots

A sure sign of the alpine community is the presence of the hoary marmot. So named for the frosty appearance of its hair, it is a champion whistler that frequently surprises high-country hikers with a loud, piercing call. So human sounding is the whistle that hikers often find themselves looking around and wondering where the other person may be.

Marmots live in small colonies and are easily found sunning themselves during July and August in boulder fields and talus slopes of mountainous country. By September, these rodents, now grown fat on vegetation and often weighing around 15 pounds, begin to sense the return of winter. Two weeks before their hibernating time they begin to fast. At the end of that time, with stomachs empty, they burrow down to a specially prepared chamber, curl up into a ball, and soon enter into such a deep sleep that they are insensitive to touch or sound.

Nature helps the marmot conserve energy. During hibernation, which may last for eight full months, the body temperature drops to just above freezing, respiration rate becomes almost imperceptible, and the heart beat grows faint. Awakening would require several hours, even if accomplished in a warm place.

In addition to the hoary marmot the yellow-bellied also occurs in Montana. More a creature of the rocky areas at lower elevations, it can be identified on the basis of habitat preferences and by the yellow underparts for which it is named.

*(a) Marmot suns itself during its relatively brief interlude from hibernation.*
*(b) Hoary marmot stands vigil near excavated maze of tunnels.*

*a*

*b*

# PORCUPINE

With 20,000 to 30,000 quills projecting from its chunky body, the likelihood of anyone mistaking the porcupine for any other animal is highly improbable. Indeed quills are the most distinctive and notorious feature of a porcupine. Individually, these structures range in size from tiny needles an inch long to matchstick-thick pins of four inches. The final length of the quill depends on its location on the animal. The longest grow on the rump, the shortest on the cheeks.

Actually, quills are no more than greatly modified hairs arising from follicles in the skin. When complete, each quill consists of three well defined parts, a solid sharp tip, usually black, a hollow white shaft, and a root similar to that of a hair. The base of each quill is connected to a layer of muscle just beneath the skin. By means of these muscles quills can be pointed rigidly upward or allowed to lie flat and at ease.

Proper manipulation of the quills protect the porcupine more efficiently than most of the defensive techniques used by many other animals. Some animals run, others hide. But the porcupine only need remain stationary and raise every quill so that all stand on end.

Other than man, the only animals that have developed the technique necessary for penetrating this armament are the cougar and fisher. According to naturalists, the fisher, with its deft coordination, manages to grab the porcupine by the tip of its tail with its teeth. Then snapping its neck upward, the fisher flips the porcupine onto its back exposing the unprotected stomach. With incredible speed, the fisher then repositions itself so that it can disembowel the porcupine with a swipe of its rapier-like claws.

One feature of the quills is that each tip is covered with many tiny barbs — similar to the ones found on a fish hook. Experiments have demonstrated that when quills and their associated barbs are placed in warm water — or warm flesh — the barbs flare away from the quill. The result is that quills work in rather than out. For the wild animal badly impaled in the facial region death is inevitable because it can't eat.

Sportsmen with hunting dogs that encounter a porcupine are best advised to seek the aid of a veterinarian. Generally dogs will have to be tranquilized. If no veterinarian is available and the number embedded in the dog are but few, an attempt to remove them by the owner may be made.

One suggested procedure for removing quills in the field is to cut off the butt end of the quill. Because quills

a

b

*Opposite Page: Passive defense is adequate for the survival of the porcupine.*

*(a) Porcupine do not hibernate during the winter and often are seen high overhead feasting on bark.*

*(b) A young porcupine sporting the same full complement of quills with which it was born.*

are hollow, this helps to collapse them. Then, with a pair of pliers, pull each out with a jerk. Because this procedure may be painful to the dog, someone should be positioned to firmly hold the dog's head and to muzzle the jaws.

Can porcupines throw their quills? Some writers have stated they can, but most mammalogists deny that they can do so at will. Old quills attached to the animal's tail help form the illusion. When the tail is given a rapid flip, inertia releases the loose quill, "throwing" it five or six feet. Certainly porcupines cannot control the shaft's trajectory or its velocity.

The porcupine's mating procedures must be rated as classic. Essentially loners, male and female porcupines manage to locate one another during the fall through a combination of urine scents and high-pitched calls. Erotic courtship displays follow the meeting during which time there is considerable muzzling, squealing and teeth chattering.

When the pair is suffcently aroused the female pulls her quills down so tightly against her back that the male's unprotected stomach is not even scratched. Needless to say, a female porcupine must be completely in agreement with the male or mating will not take place.

Young porcupines enter the world in a den usually located in the rocks along a ridge. They enter with a full complement of quills. At the time of birth, these quills are soft, but they begin to harden upon contact with the air. Within half an hour their armament is as impregnable as that of an adult, and they exhibit the same postures of defense as do their parents. It is popularly assumed that young porcupines must enter the world head first to prevent injury to the mother by backward driven quills. Orientation, however, is of little consequence, as they are still encased in one of the tough embryonic membranes common to the fetus of all mammals.

Young porcupines are fairly independent little creatures, probably because of the relatively long gestation period. Mothers carry the young for six to seven months. From infancy they can eat tender grass and herbs. By the time they are two months old, they have been weaned and are capable of surviving alone, even though they may remain with their mother until they are six months old.

Porcupines are equipped with four wood-chiseling incisors and there is little they can't eat. Much of their diet consists of bark and occasionally they girdle a tree. This preference for wood has caused some foresters to label them "pests" and they are convicted and sentenced for scarring more trees than may be warranted.

The porcupine ranges throughout the state, though it is most common in the forested mountains of western Montana. Adaptable, it has ranged over various landscapes for more than a million years. Once it was a contemporary of sabertoothed tigers and mastodons. Today, this dull witted mammal just plods along, content that as the "quill pig" it may be around for yet another million years.

41

a

b

# CHIPMUNKS

Montana has four different species of chipmunks. Although there is considerable overlap in areas of occupancy, in general, the *least* is confined to the eastern half of the state; the *yellowpine* to the western and central portions; the *red-tailed* to the Rocky Mountains; and *Uinta* to the Absaroka-Snowy and Beartooth mountain ranges.

# MUSKRAT

Because of its abundance, the muskrat has been one of the most valuable furbearing animals in Montana. Fur from this animal is used for trimming on coats, gloves and even for use by those who tie flies for fishing.

Muskrats are very prolific. A female may have two or three litters averaging five or six young in one season. As with other furbearers, established populations are self regulatory. When maximum population numbers in any one area are approached or exceeded, the incidence of predation, diseases, starvation or migration increases and limits excess growth. In a growing population, management techniques such as trapping, also may control surplus animals which become a source of income for Montana trappers, the combined total of which exceeds $20,000 each year.

In a recent 10-year period, trappers harvested almost 33,000 muskrats in Montana.

Muskrats are well adapted for their aquatic living. Broad, webbed hind feet, and a long, vertically flattened tail make them expert swimmers. Muskrats are also at home on dry land and during the spring breeding season there is considerable cross-country movement when the muskrats establish new home areas. During the mating season, muskrats are aggressive, pugnacious animals, and studies often reveal scarred noses and tails inflicted by males on one another during courtship activities, while others are received while defending private root supplies or mussel beds against other muskrats. Had they respected one another's territory, demarcated by scent deposits, such fights might never have occurred. The telltale odors, penetrating but not unpleasant, are produced by a pair of glands located near the base of the tail and are the source of the name, "muskrat."

*(a) Stripes of chipmunks extend from tail to nose.*
*(b) The least chipmunk confines itself to eastern Montana.*
*(c & d) For trappers willing to probe marshes and shallow ponds, the muskrat is a valuable furbearer.*

c

d

# HOOVED MAMMALS

Mention the word wildlife and many Montanans think of deer, sheep, elk and other animals that are included in this group of ungulates, or the hooved animals. Mention the word big game and, again, most think of animals in this group, and justifiably so. Delete the bison and add to the group discussed in this section the cougar, grizzly and black bear and you have the entire group of animals listed as Montana's big game species.

Considering only the animals classified here as hooved animals, the list is still inspiring. All members in this group are conspicuous animals that subsist on vegetation and are, in turn, preyed upon by large predators.

As vegetarians, they are considered primary consumers and they are part of a complex, relationship with the ecosystem, one that is influenced by both the environment and the availability of certain types of plants. For example, primary consumers feed on plants, which are quite abundant on Montana's vast summer ranges and, equally important, are readily available. During the winter they are forced by deep snows onto the few areas where the accumulation of snow is not so abundant. Associated with the idea of winter range is the concept of carrying capacity. For most big game populations, winter food generally is considered to be the limiting link, as animals are confined to specific areas determined by snow depth and other climatic conditions. By comparison, spring, summer and fall ranges are free from the confining aspects of deep snow and, invariably, are able to support substantially greater numbers of animals.

The areas where deer, elk and sheep congregate on winter ranges generally are located on south-facing slopes. Such areas receive more warmth from the short winter sun and, hence, snow depths are considerably less than on the north facing slopes. Montana has a number of such areas which have received so much attention that the names describing these areas have a household familiarity. What hunter or wildlife enthusiast has not heard of the Sun River or Gallatin elk herds? Less familiar are the South Fork, Blackfeet and Little Belt winter ranges. Literally dozens of these ranges occur throughout the state and all are vital in determining the number of ungulates Montana can support.

*The pronghorn is one of the many ruminants whose number is mainly governed by the amount of available winter range.*

When animals exceed the carrying capacity of these ranges, many die of starvation. The Gallatin elk herd is a famous example of this immutable fact of nature. Since the mid-'20s the herd has been permitted to overgraze its winter range and the Gallatin elk have been subjected to periodic cycles of starvation.

Many concerned citizens who have watched deer, elk and other ungulates starve to death often suggest that programs of supplemental feeding be initiated, but there are many problems associated with this solution in addition to the exhorbitant cost.

One problem is that the unfamiliar food may be initially unpalatable or distributed in such a way that it is unavailable to a sufficient number of deer in the population. Dominant deer might prevent the weaker or more needy individuals from gaining acess to the feed.

Another problem is that some period of time may be required for ungulates to learn where supplemental feed is and perhaps, to recognize it as feed. Animals with exhausted energy reserves — particularly the young of the year and the males that have drained their reserves during the rut — cannot be expected to meet these challenges.

Another major problem is that all ungulates require adjustments of the rumen microflora before optimal use can be made of the new diet. Like cattle, ungulates are ruminants; they have four compartments in their stomachs, each with a particular function.

While grazing or browsing, they swallow bits of browse, weeds and other foods. The food passes in balled-up cuds into the first "fermentation vat," the rumen. There, they mix with digestive juices containing billions of microbes. Ruminants are not born with a built-in supply of digestive microbes; they come from plants, soil and their mothers. In one way or another — or perhaps several — the young one will become inoculated with a variety of microbes. By the time it is two months old and browsing, it is well supplied. The microbes are comprised of many different species, depending on the plants a particular species may eat. Furthermore, microbes are so specialized they work efficiently on only specific foods in an animal's dietary intake. Any sudden change in foods such as introduced hay can stop the microbes' action and hasten serious complications.

a

b

c

d

But there are also "mechanical" problems to consider. Deer can starve while they continue to eat, as witnessed by many reports of dead deer found with full stomachs. The problem occurs after coarse, fibrous food is chewed and swallowed. Then the small, easily digested particles sink in the rumen fluid, where they can be attacked by microsopic bacteria in the stomach. But the large fibrous particles float on the surface of the stomach fluids where they are periodically withdrawn into another portion of the stomach. Here they are regurgitated, rechewed, and swallowed again. This process must continue until particles are broken down enough for all of their usable substance to be extracted by microbes and for the remnants to be sufficiently reduced in size to pass on to other portions of the digestive tract. If the diet is too high in fiber, a "traffic jam" develops, food intake falls, and the animal continues to be filled to capacity.

Supplemental feeding also crowds animals together creating stress and promoting the exchange of contagious diseases. Bighorn sheep are particularly susceptible to over crowding and though appearing to be healthy one day have been found dead the next.

Reproductive rates of ungulates also vary with the condition of the winter habitat. Production and survival of young ungulates is higher on good ranges than on poor ones. For example, elk calf survival and production may be nearly three times as high as areas having poor winter-range conditions. Cows on the winter ranges have a great capacity for reproduction because they are well fed. Similarly, calves that are conceived and born on ranges with adequate forage survive the hardships of winter.

The best solution then is to manage ungulates in accordance with their winter habitat. In unnatural areas, where predators have been removed for economic reasons (farming and ranching), hunters should be permitted to harvest the surplus animals produced each year. In National Parks, predators should be maintained and permitted to help the herd remain compatible with the carrying capacity of the winter range.

*(a, b, c, d) Big game managers must consider the food requirements of specific species; many ungulates have died of malnutrition with stomachs full of undigestible vegetation.*

# Mountain Goat

The world of the mountain goat is one of sharp peaks and knife-like ridges that plummet into wide valleys and deep basins dotted with azure lakes. Weather is formidable, with short summers and harsh winters, typified by blizzards which may rage for days or even weeks. Snow may pile as deep as 80 feet and wind gusts occasionally exceed 100 miles per hour. It is not uncommon for temperatures to drop to 50 degrees below zero.

Few creatures could survive in such a hostile environment, but the goat not only survives here, it is quite at home. With agile legs it defies its terrain and clings to precarious footholds, rivaling the feats of mountaineers armed with pitons, carabiners and ropes.

The mountain goat has a body that is flattened from side to side, enabling it to keep its center of gravity above the tiny ledges it traverses. In addition to the bilateral flattening, the goat's skeletal configuration allows it to draw its front and rear hooves close together to stand securely on small projections. As if that weren't enough, its short cannon bones and its unusually powerful shoulder muscles enable the goat to pull its way along rather than leaping as most other animals do.

But, perhaps the most important articles of the mountain goat's equipment are its footgear. Unusually flexible, the two toes of the goat's hooves can either spread wide apart, distributing the animal's grip over a large area, or the toes can draw together, permitting the animal to grasp minute projections. Moreover, the bottom of the hoof is made of a rough, pliable, convex traction pad edged by a hard horny shell. No wonder the goat is so secure on the sheer rock faces.

In addition to being adapted to the terrain, the mountain goat also is adapted to the extreme climate of its mountainous world. Like other alpine inhabitants, the mountain goat exhibits a shortening and thickening of the body form which minimizes surface

*Mountain goat populations probably would be safe except for the threat of back country mineral and oil development.*

a

b

c

*(a, b, c) With flexible hooves and a laterally compressed profile, the mountain goat is superbly prepared to spend its entire life in rugged mountainous terrain.*

area and consequently heat loss. The thick coat of pure white pelage also helps conserve heat. The pelage consists of a shaggy coat of hollow, eight-inch guard hairs covering a thick, fluffy layer of cashmere-quality wool. This combination of form and pelage provides the goat with protection from all but the most extreme ridgetop conditions.

In addition to its obviously adaptive morphology, the mountain goat also has behavioral adaptions that help

it survive. One is its diverse diet. Food habit studies of mountain goats have shown highly variable results. Several studies have reported shrubby browse to be the staple winter food. Others have noted dominant use of grasses and sedges. Montana writer-biologist Douglas Chadwick, who spent several winters living out of a tent observing goats from the ridges of the Swan Range, found lichens, which are removed from the rock faces with the goat's rasp-like tongue, to be of

primary importance. This adaptability is especially important in winter when the goat's mobility is limited by deep snow.

In summer, the goats prefer succulent plant tissues in the early stages of growth. Studies have shown that the nutritional value of these early growth stages of high-elevation forage is far superior to that of other available forage. Since their range is not restricted by deep snow in summer as it is in winter, the goats are able to range over a variety of exposures and elevations in search of these early physiological stages of plant growth. High quality forage is extremely important to animals having only the short alpine growing season in which to put on enough fat to survive the coming winter.

In spite of the mountain goat's adaptations to the steep terrain and the weather, these two factors are believed to be the major causes of mountain goat mortality. The largest source of mortality to adult goats appears to be accidents. Almost every day of their 12- to 13-year lives, the mountain goats are faced with the physical hazards associated with steep slopes. Rockslides, icefalls and avalanches may catch them from above; snow cornices or ledges may give way beneath them. A misplaced foot during wet or icy conditions may result in a fall and death. Of 20 goat carcasses found during a study in Glacier National Park, 12 were attributed to avalanches and three to climbing accidents.

With kids and subadults, climatic conditions appear to be the largest cause of mortality. Because of their smaller size, young goats are at a disadvantage when the snow is deep and the weather is cold. During a bad winter, a 40 percent mortality among kids and yearlings can be expected. Another cause of mortality among kids is separation from the mother. Kids tend to follow the closest large goat during sudden flight and so may occasionally become separated from their mothers.

Early records of mountain goats in Montana are rare. Lewis and Clark reported a few instances of sighting goats, and Alexander Ross reported numerous goats in the Bitterroot Valley in 1823 and 1824. The reason for this dearth of records is relatively simple. Early explorers and fur traders followed the rivers where they rarely encountered goats. To further complicate matters, existing records must be interpreted with care because, as today, goats often were confused with sheep.

The records we do have suggest that prior to 1940, mountain goats were largely unaffected by the onslaught of civilization. However, after 1940 that changed — for the better! Because goats already inhabited the major mountain ranges in the western part of the state but were absent from suitable habitat in the isolated ranges of central Montana, the Fish and Game Department began a concerted effort in 1941 to transplant goats into these isolated ranges.

The first successful transplant, in the Crazy Mountains, resulted in a hunting season there in 1953. Subsequent transplants that resulted in hunting seasons took place in the Beartooth Mountains, the Gallatin area, the Tobacco Root Mountains, the Madison Range, the Highwood Mountains, the Gates of the Mountains and the Absaroka Mountains. Less successful transplants occurred in the Snowy, Elkhorn, Highland and Bridger ranges. Today, mountain goats appear to be inhabiting all suitable habitat within the state.

Because of that trap and transplant program, there has been a five-fold increase in the opportunities for goat hunting in Montana in the past 25 years. From 1905, when the first hunting regulations for goats were established, until 1953, when a special goat hunting license was created, goats could be taken on the general hunting license. The regulations consisted largely of opening or closing areas to hunting goats. After the special license was created, the harvest from each herd could be regulated and the seasons and the harvest figures became more consistent. Because of new areas being opened to goat hunting as a result of the transplant program, the number of goats harvested each year increased until 1963 when 600 permits were sold and an estimated 513 goats were taken. Since that time, the harvest has been on a downward trend. The reduced harvest has occurred primarily in the areas with an unlimited number of permits. The harvest in the areas with limited numbers of permits has remained relatively stable.

Much research has been conducted on almost all aspects of the biology and ecology of the mountain goat although much more still can be learned about this fascinating animal.

Until very recently, the outlook for the mountain goats in Montana was considered bright. But recently, hardrock mineral development, logging, oil and gas development have altered this optimistic outlook. Several areas of Montana once thought to be free from such encroachments have suffered severe reductions in goat numbers.

Although they are often thought of as herd animals, goats really should be considered semi-gregarious. Group sizes throughout the year are consistently smaller than five animals. The largest groups occur during the summer when nursery bands are formed. These bands allow better protection of the young and

*A trap and transplant program initiated in the early '50s has placed goats in almost all available habitat.*

also allow the young to interact with each other and to begin to form the social hierarchy that becomes extremely important later on.

Social interactions within groups take place within a dominance hierarchy with the older, stronger individuals generally dominating younger, smaller animals. Aggressive adult females dominate all other classes with two-year-old males, two-year-old females, yearlings and kids following in order of increasing subordination. Adult males are effectively subordinate to other classes at times but not out of fear. When sufficiently motivated by the presence of salt or during the rut, they are capable of dominating all other classes.

Dominant animals preempt pawed feeding craters, sheltered bedsites, salt and prospective mates. They also control to some extent, the activities of the subordinate animals. In most confrontations, the underdog usually knows his place and does not resist for long, if at all. More vigorous battles may result when confrontations involve goats of similar rank.

47

# BIGHORN SHEEP

Curling majestically up form their bony core, its massive horns are without a doubt the most striking feature of the mature bighorn ram. Equal in weight to the entire skeleton, the horns may weigh up to 30 pounds or one-tenth as much as its entire body. To the ram, horns are much more than decoration or defensive weapons. They are the symbols of his social status in the herd, his physical power and his genetic fitness. Much of the ram's life within the herd is determined by his genetic capacity to produce large horns.

Born around the first of June in alpine meadows broken by steep, rugged cliffs, a male lamb begins his harried existence. Almost immediately he learns to follow his mother. Within a few days mother and young rejoin the band of ewes she left shortly before parturition. For the young, the first summer is a rather carefree time, filled with playing and cavorting.

As winter approaches, the lamb accompanies his mother and the rest of the herd to their traditional winter range. There he witnesses the head-to-head battles of older rams as they try to establish dominance, a ritual in which he will participate as he matures. The overall winner of these ritualistic battles is usually the largest horned ram in the herd. Not only does he largely determine the movements of the herd, he also can displace other sheep from the choicest forage plants, the most comfortable bedding sites, and, in the fall, the willing ewes.

Rams that have just met, or for some reason have not yet settled the dominance question, may push and shove each other as a warmup to the main event. Seeming to tire of these preliminaries, they soon turn and feed in opposite directions, seemingly oblivious to each other. Suddenly, one will turn, rear on his hind legs and propel himself at the other. Far from being surprised, the opponent performs the same maneuvers almost simultaneously and hurtles himself through the air. The adversaries may be moving at a combined speed of more than 40 miles per hour just before the moment of impact. At the last second, both rams drop from their hind legs, adding the force of gravity to their forward charge. The resulting bone-jarring crash can be heard up to a mile away. Shock

*Bighorn sheep pair near Gardiner, Montana.*

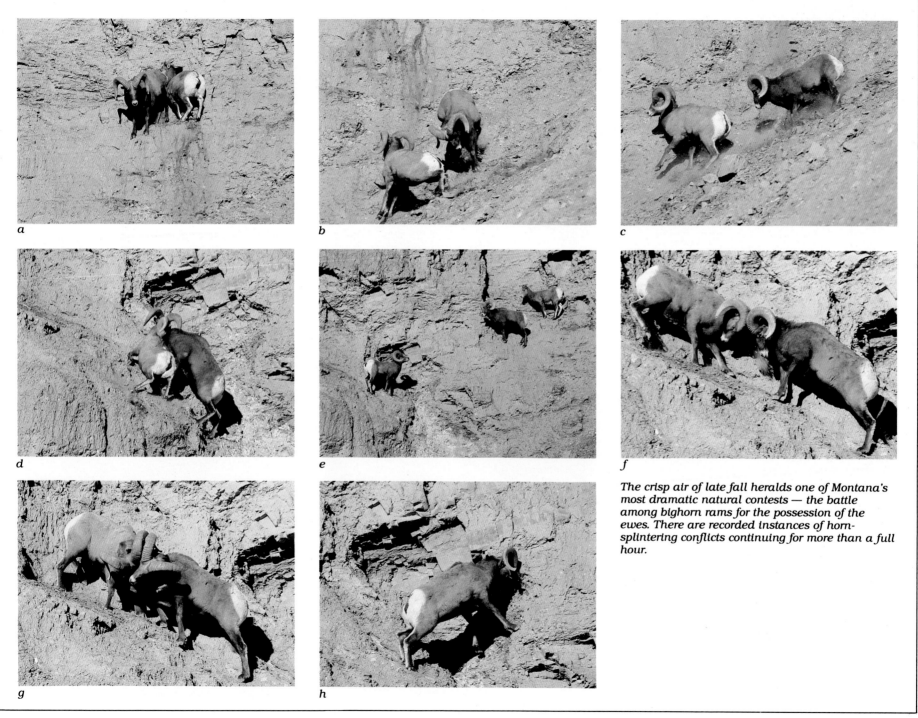

The crisp air of late fall heralds one of Montana's most dramatic natural contests — the battle among bighorn rams for the possession of the ewes. There are recorded instances of horn-splintering conflicts continuing for more than a full hour.

a

b

(a) In late December, rams in Glacier and other Montana areas appear to be on friendly terms, a far cry from the belligerent behavior of fall.

(b) Battles often are avoided when the most aggressive male gives chase to a challenger.

(c) Ram browsing on cliff face.

c

a

b

c

*(a & c) Ewe and lamb stand placidly by as rams unite in a resounding crash.*
*(b) A ram tests the receptiveness of a ewe by "flaming."*

waves from the impact ripple back over their muscular bodies, dislodging loose hair and dust. Immediately after impact, the rams raise their heads and turn them sideways, displaying their horns to full advantage. Some scientists believe this move enables each participant to equate the size of its opponent's horns with the force of the blow he has just sustained.

Bighorns are equipped to handle these blows with minimal damage. A double-layered skull supported with struts of bone, thick facial skin, and a broad, massive tendon connecting skull with spine allows the head to pivot and recoil with the blow.

Because the rams are so well protected, battles may go on for hours. Naturalists have recorded instances of evenly matched competitors clashing 48 times in a single day with no ill effects other than fatigue. Occasionally a ram will mistime the moment of impact and catch the full force of his opponent's charge on his face, resulting in a broken upper jaw, an injury that is rarely fatal. Still, biologists have discovered that rams are particularly susceptible to chronic sinusitis and other infections of the nasal passages.

The social system of the bighorn has important implications in the management of the species. Bighorns are herd animals, following age-old migration routes, and even using traditional bedding sites on their travels to and from established seasonal ranges. The herd is led by older members who learned the routes from their elders. In this way, the locations of the ranges are passed from generation to generation. Valerius Geist, a leading authority on bighorn sheep and the author of *The Mountain Sheep: A Study of Behavior and Evolution*, confirms that the "younger rams get to know the wintering areas, the salt licks, the rutting grounds, the summer ranges and the migratory ranges . . . by following the older sheep." He concludes that "sheep society is virtually designed for the passage of habits."

In the days before the settlers, when the bighorn was widespread over the mountain ranges of the state and filled all available habitat to capacity, this characteristic of sheep society was an advantage. However, with the coming of the settlers and their domestic animals, that situation changed. As more and more domestic sheep and cattle were put on the ranges, the bunchgrasses began to disappear. Limited by their social system, the bighorns were unable to move on in search of greener pastures. Instead, they continued to frequent overgrazed ranges, suffering drastic declines because of malnutrition and its accompanying diseases.

51

*(a) The horns of ewes are thinner and much shorter than those of rams.*

*(b) Kids are born in early June.*

Even now, when managers realize the importance of limiting the competition from domestic and wild animals, the social system of the sheep has limited their recovery. In areas where sheep were not completely decimated, they have recovered following the reduction of competition and accompanying range improvements. An example is the Sun River drainage which contains the largest herd found in Montana. In other areas, where no sheep survived the exploitation, restoration has been difficult. The success of trap and transplant programs into areas of suitable habitat has been limited. Surplus animals from the Sun River drainage and other transplanted herds, such as on Wild Horse Island, have been relocated in several areas of the state. In some cases, sheep transplanted in the spring on the summer range have been unable to locate the winter ranges, limiting the number of animals that survived the winter. Sheep transplanted in the fall onto their winter ranges have remained there, overgrazing the winter range and so reduce the size of the herd. Without traditional migration patterns, sheep appear to be unable to use the habitat to its fullest advantage.

One of the most successful transplant programs is the Thompson Falls herd in Sanders County. Thirteen bighorns from the Sun River herd were relocated there in May of 1959. In September of the same year, six sheep from Wildhorse Island were also released in the area. The herd since has grown to around 400 animals and currently offers some of the best trophy hunting in Montana.

Another successful transplant occurred in 1975 when 33 sheep from the Sun River sheep herd were transplanted to the Rock Creek area. An aerial survey conducted in the spring of 1982 showed the herd had proliferated and at that time numbered approximately 165 head.

Some sheephunters and biologists have brought into question the practice of harvesting only three-quarter curl or larger rams. These are the large breeding rams, the ones that sire the majority of offspring. The issue is whether the practice of removing the best animals each year is really sound management. Bighorns are the only game species that have been harvested under these trophy-biased regulations throughout their entire history. Often the analysis is drawn that a rancher would not consider removing his best bull from his herd each year. To date, there have been no studies to answer this question.

Bighorns can continue to grace our mountain slopes, but not without continued consideration from us. Management practices must be based on sound research and aimed at the preservation of the species.

# ELK

Of all the world's deer, only moose are larger than the magnificent elk. A summer fattened bull elk may weigh only 500 pounds, but 700 is more likely, and 1,000 is possible. Shoulder height is usually 4½ to 5 feet, length 7½ to 9 feet. Mature cows are a bit smaller, generally weighing between 400 and 700 pounds.

The elk is Montana's most prized big game animal from the standpoint of hunter interest, although it ranks below deer and antelope in number harvested. Today, Montana is one of the most important elk hunting states in the nation.

The hunting season begins in the fall when elk begin to drift down, but they are still in high country as the hunting season and the rut commence. At first the bulls travel in small herds or alone. Cows, calves, yearlings, and two year olds move along in herds that usually number from about 10 to 30. Soon the bulls begin to disperse; their necks swell and they begin to bugle. A bull does not gather a harem but simply takes charge of a cow herd, driving yearlings and older males out of the group. At first some of the cows break away to rejoin their adolescent offspring, but the bull drives them back with his antlers. Inevitably, rivals appear. Young ones can be scared off by a single charge. A big six-pointer will bugle and stand its ground. The adversaries circle warily, then crash together, pushing, twisting, jabbing. Most often the challenger breaks and runs.

Many confrontations are avoided by the bugling of an elk. Bugling signals an elk's territory and is one of the most thrilling sounds heard in the wilderness. Starting on a low note, it rises sharply to a clear bugle tone, then flattens to a combination of grunts and brays. A bugling elk can be heard for a considerable distance with the bellow generally being associated with the onset of the breeding season. Let other bulls beware; there is room enough for only one bull and others should stay clear.

Shortly after an elk establishes its territory and gathers its harem, breeding occurs. Calves are born in late May and early June. At birth the calves weigh from

*The monarch. For many, the elk epitomizes all that is wild and free.*

a

b

c

*(a, b, c) The elk has the adaptability to withstand dramatic fluctuations in the weather, the endurance to swim a raging river and the ready strength to engage in one of nature's most vigorous battles.*

30 to 40 pounds and may measure 3 feet long. They can walk within a matter of hours and can run when they are a week old. At that time, they also eat their first greens, but weaning is not complete until winter has descended Maturity is not reached for four years, and much growth takes place during this time.

Reproduction varies in relation to habitat conditions. If winter ranges do not contain adequate feed many young will be aborted or be inferior in strength when born. Studies by Montana biologists indicate that ratios of about 50 calves per 100 cows are indicative of favorable winter range conditions. Elk populations that traditionally have produced low cow-calf ratios are the South Fork of the Flathead herd, the Gallatin, and the Sun River herds. These ranges have been over browsed and contain insufficient nourishment to sustain a cow carrying a calf through the hardships of winter. Herds that have been compatible with their habitat and historically have produced ratios of one calf for every two cows or better are herds inhabiting the Bitterroots, Gravellys, Little Belts and the Missouri River Breaks. The continuing goal of elk management is to adjust elk populations to food supplies. Elk herds that are too large for the available winter range eventually will destroy food plants, creating erosion. A major problem in elk management is to achieve annual hunter harvests needed to adjust the number of animals to the winter range.

As with other states Montana had to learn through experience about the principles of good management. Many herds were eliminated around the turn of the century because of land-use practices and market hunting. As mentioned in previous chapters, they were hunted almost to extinction solely because of their "ivory teeth."

To re-establish herds, more than 6,000 elk have been transplanted into Montana since 1910. Most of these animals were captured in Yellowstone National Park and released in areas with suitable habitat or where it had recovered. Management tools used to create suitable areas have been fire, plant succession and logging practices. Land purchased for winter range with Pittman-Robertson funds have also helped re-establish herds. With the aid of the funds, a total of about 150,000 acres in ten different areas have been made available for elk.

An elk is one of the most wary of the big game species, and hunter success varies from virtually zero percent to about 30 percent success in Montana. A combination of luck and skill are necessary for the hunter or photographer to shoot his game.

Elk have a very keen sense of smell and persons interested in seeing them should climb high and move down through the rising thermals. Elk also have exquisite hearing; they jump at the click of a camera shutter — or a carelessly worked rifle bolt — at telephoto distances.

Elk feed actively from before dawn until mid-morning, then rest and chew their cud, sometimes feeding sporadically but not moving much until mid-afternoon. Bedding spots are often high on slopes with a wide view and rising air currents. In windy weather lee slopes and timbered ravines become equally attractive. But open areas are best on rainy or cool, humid days when elk are most active.

a

(a) Cow with a weeks-old calf.
(b) Bull bugling on a misty September morning.

b

# ELK: THE REGAL RACK

Bull elk drop their antlers in March and begin to develop a new set within a month. By July or early August, the developed, velvet-sheathed crown of a seven-year-old bull may weigh 50 pounds. As a rule, yearlings develop sizeable spikes; two and three year olds display four or five tines on each beam.

The next year's antlers generally have six long, sharp tines on each massive beam, the normal complement for a mature bull. Apart from uncommon deformities, only a relatively few great record heads display more than half a dozen tines on either side.

The main beams of an elk's rack usually sweep out, up and back, curving inward again near the tips. Almost all of those in the record book are more than four feet long and some are more than five feet.

Close to the head a long brow tine juts forward and slightly upward from each beam. A little above it is a bez tine of about equal length. The brow and bez tines together are known as lifters, dog killers, or war tines. About midway up on the beam is a tres tine, usually a little shorter than the lifters. Higher up is a fourth, called royal or dagger point, that may be more than 20 inches long. Finally, the beam tip divides into two or occasionally three tines called sur-royals, for a total of six or seven on each side. A normal six-point elk is called a royal bull or a royal stag; one with seven is an imperial. Occasionally an elk is found with eight tines on either side and such an animal is referred to as a monarch. Fully pointed at four years, annual racks grow longer and thicker through a bull's sixth, seventh, or eight-year, after which they may diminish.

A good rack is hard to judge at typical stalking distances because of the characteristic rearward sweep. If a bull holds his head low, tilting the antlers up, their length ought to be almost as great as the animal's height. If the rack is held almost horizontal, it should be about as long as the distance from the brisket to ham. From front or rear, it may not look very high, but it should look massive and considerably wider than the bull's body.

*(a) Royal elk with antlers that may weigh 50 pounds.*

*(b) Cooling down.*

*(c) Bull elk with small harem.*

a

b

c

# MULE DEER

When the mule deer perks up its head and the great ears twist forward, the reason for the name is apparent. His mule ears are a quarter again larger than those of the whitetail.

As it plods along with ears flapping, it is not nearly as shapely as the whitetail. The body seems heavy and the legs stocky and less trim. Even the feet are larger. But when something startles the animal, it becomes vibrant, alive, and graceful. The head comes up, and it vaults away with high leaps that seem to be powered by coiled springs. When alarmed, the mule deer has been known to jump eight feet from a running start of only a few feet. For a few minutes, it can run 35 miles per hour. Little wonder it received so much attention from early explorers.

Apparently the first explorers to encounter the mule deer were Lewis and Clark, and there is evidence they coined the name. In his Journal Lewis wrote: "We have rarely found the mule deer in any except rough country. They prefer the open grounds and are seldom found in woodlands or rough bottoms."

As with many other forms of wildlife discussed in the opening sections, mule deer were generally scarce during the mid-'30s. Today, however, as noted in a Montana Department of Fish, Wildlife and Parks publication, mule deer occur: ". . . from Yaak to Alzada and from Monida to Westby and on almost every square mile in between. They are found at all elevations from under 3,000 feet on sagebrush flats in eastern Montana to over 8,000 feet in western Montana." Other fish and game literature, however, also points out that the stability of populations within specific areas is cyclical and uncertain. The uncertainty arises because of land-use practices, and as one biologist said of the large mule deer herd roaming the Missouri breaks: "At this point it is difficult to determine whether trends since the 1960s represent only periodic ups and downs in a generally stable population, or the beginnings of a long-term decline which may continue as habitat diminishes and land-use patterns change."

The mule deer is not as timorous as it looks. The buck as well as the doe often takes after hungry coyotes and drive them away. If angry enough, it may jump on an over-rash coyote with all four feet until the predator is dead or at least its bones broken. The same applies to human intruders, and the writers are familiar with one incident which resulted in a Glacier Park Ranger having had his abdominal cavity opened by flying hooves.

a

b

c

(a, b, c) As biologists like to say, mule deer in Montana now occupy all available habitat from Yaak to Alzada.

59

a

b

During the rut, the mule deer buck does more bluffing and less actual fighting than the male whitetail. When he eventually selects a mate, he wastes little time on an unwilling female. Scent tells him when a doe is ready and he gives chase through the densest of forests until he finds her. Occasionally an enterprising buck acquires a harem of three or four does. The does may leave or stay, but generally prefer to stay. Rivals are quickly chased away, unless they look bigger and stronger.

By the middle of December deer have settled down to the quiet routine of winter. The bucks become thin and spiritless, and a few weeks afterward, they lose their antlers. The young bucks with only spikes may hold onto them a few weeks longer.

Mule deer are migratory and typically use different summer and winter ranges. Summer is spent in the mountains where fields of flowers cover alpine meadows. Winter is spent in the valleys where food is still available and where their movements are not hampered by deep snow. Montana biologists have recorded instances where radio collared deer have covered 300 miles on their annual round-trip jaunt from summer to winter quarters.

Fawns are born in late June or early July, soon after the does reach the summer range. Most does have twins and occasionally triplets, although young mothers and those in poor condition generally have only one. The little animals weigh six to seven pounds at birth. When about a month old they are strong enough to run with their mothers.

The cougar is the most important natural enemy of the mule deer and in some areas may account for the death of one deer every 10 to 14 days, particularly in the winter. Few other animals have the strength and cunning to stalk a healthy deer on a routine basis, although during crusty snow conditions in winter, coyotes may become effective predators on deer.

The dichotomously branching antlers of the mule deer are greatly prized as trophies. Normally, a full head has a total of 10 tines, although abnormal sets of antlers have been recorded with 60 or more points. The largest head ever taken in the United States with a regulation set of tines scored 225¾ in the Boone and Crockett record book. The animal, which was harvested in Dolores County, Colorado, measured 33¾ inches along the outside curve of the beam, and tallied nine points. The largest every taken in Montana was harvested in Ravalli County by Sherman L. Williams in 1978, scoring 201½ inches in the Boone and Crockett record book. Its main beams were 28⅛ inches and 28⅜ inches with an inside spread of 22⅞ inches. One side had five points, the other seven.

*(a) Mule deer in rut. Note swollen neck.*

*(b) Mule deer can be recognized by their ears which are a quarter again as large as those of the whitetail.*

# White-Tailed Deer

During the 15 or 20 million years since the forebearers of the American whitetail crossed the land bridge from Asia, it has developed into a unique species found nowhere else in the world. During the intervening time, deer have been subjected to nature's experimentation in a constantly changing environment and exposed to ecological, geological and climatic disturbances. These tests have finely honed their ability to adjust to transitory conditions. Even so, whitetails were almost brought to the brink of extinction by change, and their story is one of near tragedy.

By the turn of the century the clearing of agricultural lands and the cutting of timber promoted population growth that soared. Then a decline set in, partly because of uncontrolled slash fires and forest fires, and the abandonment of ravaged lands as lumbermen moved westward. The second-growth trees and shrubs, sprouting on heavily lumbered tracts, eventually grew so tall that shade-intolerant browse was cut off. These climax forests, with little browse, could not support deer herds. Simultaneously, settlers were massacring deer for food, hides, and the protection of crops. At one time, hides were considered legal tender in Montana, and, as a market developed for skins, the slaughter accelerated.

But the crisis precipitated an unprecedented conservation movement. A restocking program was initiated in the '30s and '40s and some states subsequently have become famous for populations that grew from these nucleus herds.

In some of these areas, the animals were protected fully for many years and in others, hunting was restricted to antlered bucks. Simultaneously, suitable habitat was recreated.

Today, for the very same reasons deer populations were jeopardized in the early 1900s, the continued existence of some of Montana's whitetail herds is uncertain.

*Though whitetails are found on more than 38,000 square miles of state land, their numbers once again may be threatened.*

When attempting to encourage the growth of white-tail deer populations, land-use patterns must be considered. Farmers in eastern Montana are under the stress of increasing costs and must make every acre produce the highest number of bushels per acre or face ultimate bankruptcy. Uncultivated lands lying fallow is a luxury the farmer cannot afford. As a result, wooded areas, brushy draws, and other areas important to whitetails are being converted to crop land. the small farmer has no alternative if he is to survive with today's competitive markets.

In western Montana, the story is not much more encouraging. Intensive studies conducted by biologists in the Swan Valley indicate that one of the most important factors affecting whitetail deer range is fire. The low shrubs that follow a fire create favorable deer habitat. In lieu of fires, certain types of logging operations also have proven beneficial to whitetails on certain sites.

The Swan Valley is an example of one Montana area where such conditions have not been practiced or permitted to occur. As a result deer hunter-harvest surveys indicate fewer deer are now being taken by hunters in areas of Montana where climax forests exist.

Whitetail deer challenge a hunter's abilities as much as any North American game species. They are cunning in their ability to protect themselves. When disturbed they feed at night and remain hidden during the day. During hunting season, they use their stealth in avoiding hunters more effectively than do many other big game species. As a result, few hunters return with venison and few photographers return with pictures. But there are two factors that favor the outdoor person looking for whitetails.

The first is that within the small home range most deer repeatedly use the same routes between bedding and feeding areas. A heavily used deer run is well marked with tracks and droppings, and sometimes becomes grooved from trampling.

For the hunter, the second advantage is that, in most areas, the hunting season coincides with at least part of the breeding season. A rutting buck, preoccupied with finding does and challenging rivals, loses some of his caution. And by moving about in daylight more than at other times, the buck increases his chances of being spotted or ambushed.

Once it was thought a third factor existed that might assist the hunter interested in locating whitetails. Previously it was believed that white-tailed deer utilized the same area as their summer and winter range. Recently this assumptions has been disproved.

a

b

c

a

*Opposite Page: (a) Whitetail deer showing the "white flag" of warning. (b & c) Whitetail fawns. This Page: (a & b) Whitetail bucks have one main beam from which rise individual tines.*

b

a

b

In the Swan, radio telemetry has demonstrated whitetails do have distinctly different summer and winter ranges and may, on occasion, travel considerable distances to reach these areas. In one extreme example, Biologist John Mundinger recorded the signals from a radio-collared deer that had traveled from Goat Creek in the Swan Valley over two mountain ranges and established herself near Scott Lake adjacent to the Middle Fork of the Flathead, a distance of 35 air miles.

Even more dramatic is the deer that was tracked from Salmon Lake in mid December back to Goat Creek by January first — a distance of 53 miles in less than two weeks. Obviously, white-tailed deer do migrate and occasionally over a considerable distance.

Montana always has had a population of whitetail deer and their presence was documented in the Journals of Lewis and Clark, who first noted them in the vicinity of the Poplar River. Whitetails hardly were mentioned again until the explorers reached the three forks of the Missouri River. As in other states, their story represents somewhat of a conservation milestone.

Traditionally, Montana whitetails have inhabited river bottoms found east of the Continental Divide. But prior to the 1940s, they had disappeared from much of their historic range. Since 1941, whitetails gradually have extended their range and are now found on more than 38,000 square miles in eastern and western Montana. As a species they have proved to be one of the most adaptable of mammals and with the good management that followed the encouragement of an incensed public, have managed to reestablish themselves over age-old lands. Today they are found from coast to coast and from the latitude of Hudson Bay in Canada, south to the Isthmus of Panama. Whether they continue to thrive in Montana is essentially up to the public. Using finances only as the criteria for preserving them in all of their native haunts represents a valid argument; they represent a potential for recreational hunting that has not reached its capacity. As one biologist said, "If we can succeed in improving the poor ranges and maintaining the good ones, we can expect to have whitetails in Montana indefinitely."

*Radio telemetry studies conducted recently have shown that whitetails may migrate considerable distances, contrary to prevailing thought that they mostly stay in home territory. In the Swan Range, several have covered distances of 50 air miles.*

# MOOSE

The moose is the largest antlered deer ever to have stalked the face of the earth. Fossil finds have revealed moose with twice the girth of those found today, though these still have considerable stature. A mature 20th-century bull weighs from 1,000 to 1,400 pounds or so. A cow weighs from 600 to 800 pounds.

A fine bull moose grows heavier antlers than any other living mammal. A record "head" may spread 70 inches or more. One of the largest heads taken in Montana had antlers with a spread of 58½ inches. The broad sweeping shovels, with their many short prongs along the front edge and outer end, are magnificent. They are among the most prized of all hunting trophies.

Earliest written accounts of moose in Montana come from the Journals of Lewis and Clark. Hunters in the party encountered moose while ascending the Missouri a few miles above the mouth of Montana's Milk River and again while camped near the present location of Lincoln.

Historical writings indicate that current moose distribution in Montana probably differs little from when white men first visited the region. They are localized in distribution, except in the northwest corner. While they are not abundant in many areas, moose do, however, occur in most of the mountain ranges of western and central Montana.

Moose populations in the state have varied considerably in the last 100 years. In the 1900s they were virtually extinct, though 10 years later records indicate they rebounded.

Intensive scientific studies of moose were initiated in Yellowstone National Park in 1947. Two Montana studies began in 1958, one in the upper Ruby River area. These and subsequent studies provide most of the information for managing Montana's moose.

In addition to the experience of the hunt, there may be the reward of up to 700 pounds of delicious meat. It

*Lewis and Clark provided the first written accounts of Montana moose, which they encountered near the mouth of the Milk River.*

a

b

c

*(a, b, c) Who can place a monetary value on the experience of seeing a moose in the wild?*

*Opposite: Moose in fall rut.*

is impossible to place a value on the experience of observing or photographing a bull moose in his prime standing in solitary assuredness, or a cow moose quietly leading her twin calves through a forest.

As with other big game species, the primary problem moose managers face today and in the future is the maintenance of adequate habitat. Knowledge of the particular ecological requirements of each moose population and the associated species of animals pasturing on the same range is also essential to sound management and the establishment of realistic quotas. Under current harvest conditions hunters can become eligible each year if their permit is pulled in a chance drawing.

Most hunters consider moose the toughest antlered trophy to judge, even when a bull stands in the open. A moose is apt to be eight to 10 feet long from nose to tail and at its shoulder 5½ to 7½ feet high. Its rack, 8 to 10 feet above its enormous hoofs, looks inadequate. A front or rear view helps, for a good rack hangs far out, about twice as wide as the chest. The legs, adapted for wading, are often more than 40 inches long. If a bull is seen in profile, professional guides advise clients that the antlers ought to shade the body and a portion of the neck. The small points, edging the palms, will probably be impossible to count.

Hanging down from the massive head about six inches below his throat is the bell or rope-like flap of skin covered with long hair which has no apparent function. This varies in length from a few inches to 3 feet, 12 to 15 inches being average. Reaching its best development in young bulls, it becomes a mere dewlap in old animals. The cow's bell is generally smaller.

Moose are strong swimmers though no one knows how far they can travel by this means. Moose have been seen swimming portions of Yellowstone Lake, which spans about eight miles. Occasionally moose drown when swimming and sometimes they break through thin ice and are unable to regain the shore.

During the rut, the bull moose is likely to become very disagreeable. He has driven many a man up a tree and kept him there, sometimes for hours. "Nature Notes," maintained by Yellowstone National Park, tell of a few instances where an irate moose has charged a moving vehicle.

During the rut, cows are very aggressive toward one another. In contrast to other antlered species, they assume an active and independent role during the rut and may aggressively seek out rutting males. They may also advertise their presence through the use of vocal signals. Sounds produced by females have been described by mammalogists as "a long quavering moan."

*a*

*b*

With all their power it is not surprising to learn that in Europe, the moose was at times used as a draft horse. In a few cases, the American moose has also been broken to harness.

*Moose often feed on aquatic plant life with heads completely submerged for several minutes.*

*c*

# PRONGHORN

An old Blackfoot legend recounts how the pronghorn was created. The "Old Man," the Blackfoot god, made the pronghorn out of dirt while he was in the mountains. When he finished, the Old Man turned his creation loose to see how well it could run. The pronghorn took off so fast it immediately tripped over some rocks and hurt itself. Then the Old Man decided to take it to the prairie to see how it fared there. When the pronghorn negotiated the prairie with a great deal of speed and grace, the Old Man was very pleased, convinced that the pronghorn was best suited for the open plains.

With eyesight that has been likened to that of a man aided by seven-power binoculars, slim legs that carry him over the ground faster than any other North American mammal, and an enlarged windpipe and oversize lungs and heart that contribute to an endurance unexcelled by man or beast, the pronghorn is indeed an animal that is best suited to the open plains.

The first white man to see the pronghorn is believed to be the Spanish explorer, Francisco Vasquez Coronado. He made a trip north of Mexico into what is now New Mexico and Kansas around 1540. His description of pronghorn was "stags patched with white."

It was not until after the Lewis and Clark expedition of 1804-1806 brought back a specimen that the pronghorn received its scientific name. George Ord, a zoologist of that time, named the pronghorn *Antilocapra americana*. Translated from the Latin, the name means American goat-antelope. In actuality, the pronghorn is neither a goat nor an antelope. Because its forked horns are unique, it has been placed in a family of its own, the Antilocapridae.

The pronghorn flourished until early settlers began turning over the thick prairie sod. Many experts estimated their number west of the Mississippi in excess of 40 million, including the two and one-half million animals in Montana. By the 1920s, the indiscriminate shooting and loss of habitat had taken their toll and the once great herds of pronghorn dwindled to a mere 15,000 in the country with about 3,000 remaining here in this state.

*Pronghorn at alert on the Moiese Bison Range.*

About that time, wardens were hired to enforce the hunting laws and the great depression turned the dreams of many homesteaders into dust as their crops failed. As the pioneers abandoned their farms along with their hopes and dreams, the prairie sod began to heal. With that, the pronghorn began its comeback. Today, there are an estimated 100,000 pronghorn in the state, more than at any other time in this century.

Like the young of other ungulates, pronghorn fawns are born in the spring, usually in late May or early June. Sometime before her time arrives, the doe isolates herself from the rest of the herd. Shortly before the birth, she selects a secluded spot in which she can escape detection by predators. As fawning becomes inevitable, the doe begins to act very nervous. She may lie down, rise, lie down and then jump to her feet again. The actual birth may occur while she is either standing or lying down. About 60 percent of first pregnancies result in twins. Subsequent pregnancies almost invariably result in twins.

Immediately after giving birth, the doe carefully grooms the fawn. She licks the gangly creature meticulously from head to hoof, a procedure that is crucial in the establishment of the bond between the doe and her fawn.

Within half an hour, the fawn has battled its way to its feet, but, everytime the mother nuzzles it, no matter how gently, balance is lost and it collapses to the ground. Within an hour after birth, through a process of trial and error, the fawn has found its mother's udder. Nursing for less than a minute before going on to other things, but it will come back as many as eight times within the first three hours.

After nursing, the fawn wanders off, selects a bed and lies down. The doe moves off to graze and rest. For the next few days, the fawn will spend from 20 to 22 hours a day sleeping by itself.

Although the fawn is unable to defend itself or outdistance predators during these first few days, it is not totally at the mercy of its enemies. Its drab coloration blends well with the soil and the prairie plant life, making it difficult to see. Instinctively it freezes at any unusual sight, sound or scent, further helping it escape detection. During the first few days of its life there is an

*In June, female antelope search for a secluded area where they give birth to their young. Within an hour, young are on their feet and capable of running short distances.*

*Opposite Page:*
*Bucks gather harems which they defend vigorously against other interested males.*

a

c

b

*d*

*c*

*a*

*b*

71

a

b

*Fleetest of all the ungulates, pronghorns have been clocked at speeds approaching 50 miles per hour.*

absence of any detectible odor. Hunting dogs have been known to walk within inches of motionless fawns without discovering them.

The fawn rapidly develops its running abilities. The first day or two it is still shakey and awkward, but by the third day it can outrun a man, and after a week it can run smoothly and effortlessly. At two weeks of age, the fawn can cover ground at the rate of 35 miles per hour.

After the fawn is able to keep up with its mother, the two rejoin the growing herd of does and fawns. The fawn begins playing with other fawns, taking part in various pronghorn games vital to muscular development and coordination. These games take the form of running in circles, chasing each other, butting heads and generally rough-housing with the other fawns and its mother. It is during these games that the fawn begins to establish its place in the hierarchy of the herd that will be a part of its life from that time on.

In spite of the attention of the doe and the youngster's rapid growth and remarkable ability to fend for itself, mortality among fawns is very high. By the first of September, as many as half of the fawns born in the spring may be dead. The reasons for this high mortality rate are many. Drought, disease, parasites, congenital defects and predators may contribute to substantial losses.

Without a doubt, the worst enemy of the pronghorn is winter. Well fed pronghorn are in little danger from the often severe and punishing winters of eastern Montana. Their coarse, brittle hair is hollow, providing much better insulation against the extreme cold than one might suspect at first glance. In addition to the 2-inch outer coat of hair, the pronghorn has an inner coat of very fine hair that also increases its insulating ability. A complex system of muscles just under the skin allows the animal to raise or lower its hair to control the escape of air depending on the outside temperature.

Many biologists and photographers have bundled in down clothing to accompany pronghorn on a subzero day, only to give up in utter agony while the pronghorn went about their business, oblivious to the cold.

While they have adequate outer-wear for winter, pronghorn also need fuel for their internal furnaces. In Montana, that fuel takes the form of sagebrush. Antelope migrate to the same places each winter and stay until spring. The common factor in most of those winter ranges is an adequate amount of sagebrush.

In areas of adequate sagebrush, such as along the Milk River from Havre to Glasgow, the problem can be readily observed. During the winter of 1964-65, the most severe ever recorded in Montana, below zero temperatures were recorded in Glasgow for 78 consecutive days. Snows reached depths of 40 inches and the wind blew constantly. Five hundred pronghorn died of starvation in addition to several hundred that were killed by cars and trains as they rested on or crossed roads and railroad tracks. Biologists examining carcasses discovered that 97 percent of the animals were in the advanced stages of malnutrition.

That same year, the weather on the pronghorn winter range near Malta was comparable to that near Glasgow. Yet, the losses were minor. The difference was the presence of adequate sagebrush. Between 4,000 and 5,000 pronghorn survived the winter on a stretch of sagebrush one mile wide and 15 miles long!

The goal of managers in Montana is to match pronghorn numbers with the quantity and quality of winter range through the use of hunter harvest quotas. This is relatively easy compared to the greater and more important task of preserving critical winter range. Without adequate winter range, pronghorn will not be able to survive in the same numbers we now have.

Upon seeing the pronghorn for the first time in 1843 painter-naturalist John James Audubon wrote, during a trip on the Missouri river: "Hurrah for the prairies and the swift antelope. They fleet by the hunter like flashes or meteors. They pass along, up or down hills, or along the level plain with the same apparent ease, while so rapidly do their legs perform their graceful movements . . . that like the spokes of a fast turning wheel we can hardly see them, but instead observe a gauzy or film-like appearance." May it always be so.

*No matter the distortion, horns are retained throughout life.*

## HORNS OR ANTLERS

One of the biggest differences between the two structures is that antlers are grown and shed every single year. Horns are not. They stay with the animal its entire life. The only animal in North America that confounds this rule is the pronghorn. Only pronghorn shed their horns as if they were antlers, though only the outer horny sheath, not the bony core. It is the only animal in the world with horns that branch. Female pronghorn also have horns but like most sheep and goats, they maintain their growths throughout the year.

Antlers begin to grow during the spring of each year and then fall off sometime during the winter, depending upon the particular species. The growth of antlers places a great deal of strain on the animals producing them. These structures begin their growth from two small "roots" located on the front of the head. With the exception of caribou only males produce them, and they generally are used for fighting other males. Velvet helps them to grow.

Velvet is nothing more than skin and blood vessels which surround the antlers as they begin to grow each spring. The substance is there to provide antlers with nourishment as they grow larger through the year. In the fall, velvet begins to itch, so the animal rubs it off. If you see an animal at this time of the year, you may see the velvet hanging down like moss from trees in a rain forest. Several weeks later it is gone and, at this time, antlers are polished by the male until they glitter and shine. They are ready for use during the mating season to protect a male's harem or in the defense of territory.

Antlers and horns differ in composition. Antlers are made of bone; horns from a material known as keratin, which is found in other parts of mammals in their hooves, hair, claws and fingernails.

Horns are grown by both males and females and, in their early stages of growth, are soft and may be damaged. The result may produce unusual growth patterns such as the one shown by the ewe in the accompanying photograph.

Horns of sheep and goats also tell something about the age of an animal. If you get close to one, you'll see a series of lines. These lines are like the rings in a tree and, if you count them, they will tell you the number of years the animal has been around.

## TRANSPLANTING

In 1970, the Department of Interior published a report entitled "Islands of America," listing what the agency considered the most significant islands in the nation.

Wild Horse Island was mentioned. And if you have ever driven U.S. 93 between Polson and Kalispell, lingering near Dayton, you may understand why.

Looking to the east, you see an island surrounded by some of the most magnificent country in the world. The island in Flathead Lake, the largest natural fresh water lake in the West, is bordered to the east and north by the Swan and Mission mountain ranges.

But if there is a single romantic bone in your body, your eyes will drift back to the island. It is remote and appears as though it might not ever have been visited. But that is a delusion because the island has a history that includes Indians, homesteaders, developers, conservationists, state and federal intervention, a state fish and game management plan and wild horses. Wild Horse Island has served as the staging area for one of the state's greatest wildlife controversies sparking angry public sentiment and culminating in one of the largest transplant programs to have occurred in recent years.

The stage for the problem began in 1939 when one male and one female sheep were planted on the island. Sheep have never been native to the island but the majority of public sentiment today reflects the feelings of wildlife enthusiasts in the late '30s — so much native sheep habitat had been destroyed by the encroachment of civilization that these animals should be preserved wherever suitable habitat can be found.

In 1949, the Montana Department of Fish and Game planted four more sheep. From these modest numbers the population proliferated; in 1972, the sheep population was estimated at the incredibly high number of 309.

In the late 1970s the island's sheep population was in serious trouble. The winter range showed ample evidence of sustained overuse: shrubs were all but gone, the reproduction of conifer trees was nonexistent, and invading plant species such as cheat grass were abundant. Obviously, the animals were not in balance with their environment. The result was that in 1978 more than 40 sheep, mostly mature rams, died during the valley's severe winter. The public was incensed. Wildlife protectors wanted a sustained feeding program; hunters wanted to harvest the surplus. A bitter debate ensued, which eventually was resolved by a transplant program.

In 1978 and 1979 several hundred sheep were transplanted by helicopter to other state locations. Left behind by the Montana Fish and Game department were 75 sheep, the number believed to be the carrying capacity of the island. Today these sheep will be maintained at somewhere below 100. Surplus sheep will not be hunted, rather they will serve as seed stock for new sites or as a source of recruitment for older herds.

# Profile of a Predator

The skull of the cougar pictured at left epitomizes the many animals predator control officers — hired not only by the state of Montana, but also by the National Park Service — attempted to eliminate between 1872 and 1930. During that period, the principles of wildlife management were in their infancy, and the lesson of a lingering agony inflicted on deer and elk by starvation from the depletion of forage on overgrazed ranges had to be demonstrated before conservation agencies could envision the reality of the predators and hunters harvesting the surplus crop produced annually.

Certainly predators help provide this balance, and there is nothing lingering about the death exacted by a predator. Nature has endowed these animals with the means of dispatching prey swiftly and surely. Death is almost certain, and it generally is instantaneous.

Examine the teeth in the photograph of the cougar skull, little escapes their bite. With canines several inches long, it is apparent that they are designed for tearing. Molars, too, are formed differently from yours and mine; a side view would show that, unlike the grinding teeth of humans or deer, the molars of carnivores act like scissors; they are excellent for shearing.

Human hunters help harvest excess numbers of ungulates, but they cannot produce the same beneficial effects as four-footed predators, even if there were more of them and the hunting seasons were longer. By taking the most vulnerable animals in a population, the old, young, sickly, and ill-adapted — in a very simplified sense predators keep the herd genetically sound. The result is all profit; not only for prey and predator, but also for the human hunter. The two-footed predator profits from the availability of game that is stronger, larger, more perceptive and more challenging.

*(a) Cougar skull revealing teeth that shear and tear.*

*(b, c) Labeled glutton, Indian devil, wolf marten, it's more commonly known as the wolverine.*

# FLESH EATERS

## COYOTE — THE SONG DOG

Frank Dobie wrote in his classic book *Voice of the Coyote*, "If I could, I would go to bed every night with coyote voices in my ears and with them greet the gray light of every dawn. When I remember their derision of campfires, their salutes to the rising moon, their kinship cries to stars and silences, I am ten thousand times more grateful to them than I am to the makers of the blaring radios and ringing telephones that index the high standard of American living."

Despite the romantic appeal of the coyote in literature, few animals have been maligned more than the coyote. Because of its nature it generates controversy and, as one Montana biologist said, "Anyone in eastern Montana old enough to drive a pickup has an opinion about coyotes." And little wonder. From the staid offices of scientific researchers come tomes of published documentations sufficient to reinforce the stand anyone may care to take. Say the researchers: "Coyotes play a measureable part in regulating deer numbers but do not control rodents." Or, "coyotes cannot regulate deer populations but can efficiently reduce rodents." Or, "predator control invariably leads to the substantial increase in wildlife." And now finally after years of study we find the Montana Department of Fish, Wildlife and Parks saying: "At present and with existing conditions, coyote control solely to benefit big game in Montana can neither be justified nor recommended."

Without further elaboration the advice seems sound, and since the authors are old enough to drive a pickup we believe that as hunters we too can offer an opinion. But it is based on prejudice — the prejudice of one who has heard the plaintive wail of the coyote as it drifts across the sprawling prairie and heard it as it reverberates between escarpments along the Missouri River. The song dog should stay to help sheep herders keep their flocks in order and help nurture the ire of hunters.

The name coyote apparently originated with the Aztec Indians and was passed on, with considerable modification, by the Spaniards. Its Latin or scientific name is *Canis latrans*, but it has been known locally

a

c

*(a) Persecuted until extinct from Montana, migrant wolves have recently been seen in the North Fork region of Glacier National Park.*

*(b) Fully aware of the presence of the coyote (lower right), a band of sheep passes. The main threat is to young or sick animals that might be separated from the band. The test is a long chase.*

*(c) A cunning and adaptable scavenger, the coyote is loathed by many. Still, it remains the song dog whose mournful wail stirs the imagination.*

b

a

b

by such names as the prairie wolf, brush wolf and cased wolf. The name cased wolf was an old trade name. Coyote hides were cured cased — that is, they were peeled off the carcasses like a glove during skinning. In contrast, an open pelt was one that had been cut open along the belly and could be spread flat. This is the way the true wolves were pelted. Coyotes are small animals, smaller in weight than it may appear to most persons. It averages 30 pounds and is only about six feet long from pointed nose to the tip of its bushy tail.

A number of misconceptions surround this little canine, but perhaps the most prevalent and recurring one is that they take more than their fair share of game animals. Recent studies conducted by the Montana Department of Fish, Wildlife and Parks indicate this is a fallacy. To arrive at this conclusion, the Department established three study areas in the early '70s primarily to provide an answer to the many who already had made up their minds that predators are the sole reason Montanans don't have an unlimited supply of many species of game birds and mammals. The data, however, do not confirm this assumption. In short, biologist Phillip Schladweiler reconfirmed that human-caused coyote mortality simply replaces natural mortality. Each species of wildlife, he noted, must produce a large excess of young each spring to compensate for natural attrition which may occur from factors such as competition within the brood. This depletion in a population occurs whether or not man intervenes. Furthermore, if control exceeds natural mortality, remaining coyotes become better fed, survive better, and reproduce at a higher rate."

Schladweiler concludes: "At present and with existing conditions, coyote control solely to benefit big game in Montana can neither be justified nor recommended . . . The economics of control efforts versus produced benefits must be the major consideration — the hunter's money should be spent where it most benefits the hunter." Among other factors that also should be balanced against the coyote's food habits are recreational and trapping values. In years when pelts from these animals are in fashion, coyotes provide a source of income to trappers. Hunters also enjoy pitting their skills against coyotes by using predator calls; it is one method biologists suggest the public might use for reducing the number of coyotes.

Realizing the adaptability of the coyote, it is not surprising that its family life also may vary. No two pairs follow any given pattern. Home for the pair may be a tree in a forest, a hollow log, a cave in a cliff, a space in a pile of rocks or a burrow in the ground. Mating takes place from February through April and the gestation period is from 60 to 65 days. Litters average around six pups, though the number may vary considerably.

As a rule, coyotes mate for life and generally are devoted to one another. They have been known to bring their mates food if bound by a trap. When the female is pregnant, the male provides. If we approach too closely, one parent will attempt to decoy us away. Enos Mills attests to this fact. In an interview in the late 1800s, the famous naturalist commented on the commonly known effort of parent coyotes to divert human beings from a den. Then he added, "I have also seen one or more coyotes stay near a crippled coyote as though taking care of it, and attempt to lure away any hunter who approached."

Because of these traits, we are the richer. Without them the coyote might have perished long ago. But today the "song dog" lives, seldom seen, but often heard — at least that's true of Montana where it can still wail — though not always to its heart's content.

c

*(a & b) An acute sense of hearing enables the coyote to detect the scurry of a mouse — even beneath a cloak of snow.*

*(c) Wolves are almost twice again as large as their close cousin, the coyote.*

a

b

*Red fox foursome.*

d

c

# MOUNTAIN LION

As the trail became hotter, the tempo of the hound chorus rose to a peak of wild yelping and barking. Two hunters trailed far behind, laboring through snow two feet deep, and wincing as the raw, subzero air whistled into their burning lungs.

A change in the baying of the hounds signaled that the animal had been treed and this spurred the two men to even greater efforts. Finally, two tortuous hours after first striking the trail, the duo saw their quarry. Forty feet up in an old pine tree, a cougar watched the dogs with piercing eyes. Spotting the approaching men, the big cat swapped ends. Facing them, it hissed and swatted the air.

After catching and leashing the clamoring hounds, the men admired the lion for a few moments, recounted the exciting chase, and began the long trek back to their vehicle, their tired but still eager dogs in tow.

Scenes similar to this take place in Montana many times each winter. Killing cats is allowed only during the first part of the lion season which extends from about the beginning of December to the end of April. However, many houndsmen, dedicated to the welfare of the lion, refrain from filling their tags. This self restraint ensures moderate harvests of cougars in the state and allows a liberal lion management system unequaled in most other western states. Currently, between 50 and 100 lions are taken annually in Montana, most of them from the timbered slopes west of the Divide.

Thanks to these dedicated sportsmen and a system of enlightened management, this animal, described by Ernest Thompson Seton as a "lithe and splendid beasthood," seems secure in its Montana environs. Numbers of cougars in the western and central parts of the state appear to be stable and may be increasing. In addition, the cougar seems to be expanding its range in the east.

Although it is now regarded as a necessary and highly desirable part of the ecosystem, the cougar was once thought of as vermin. Even the conservation-minded Teddy Roosevelt described the cougar as a "big horse-killing cat, destroyer of deer and lord of stealthy murder . . . with a heart craven and cruel." Looked on as a competitor for deer and other game, it was indiscriminately destroyed by shooting, trapping, poisoning and any other possible means. A bounty of up to $50 per hide was paid here in Montana until 1962. The cougar was declared a game animal in 1971 and hunting has been carefully regulated since then.

Even though they are relatively common throughout western Montana, and can be found in the Missouri River breaks and other parts of eastern Montana, cougars are seldom seen by anyone without the aid of dogs. Their nocturnal habits and shy secretive nature allow them to live at the edge of civilization without being detected.

This ability to skulk about unseen is essential to a cougar because it lives by capturing and killing wary prey. Sharp eyes and a keen nose locate its next meal. Short, muscular legs and a supple body enable the big cat to take advantage of every shred of available cover to escape detection by the ever vigilant eyes. Padded feed allow it to move noiselessly through even brittle undergrowth and avoid detection by radar-like ears while positioning itself for the final assault.

Propelled by powerful hind legs, the cougar bursts from cover and overtakes its startled prey with a short sprint of blazing speed. Strong shoulders and forelegs help it strike and hold the animal while needle-like retractable claws dig into the sides and back of its prey. Long, strong canine teeth, powered by muscular jaws, disjoint the vertebrae with a swift bone-crushing bite at the base of the skull. Death is almost instantaneous.

After the kill, the cougar may drag the carcass for a considerable distance, even over rough terrain, before feeding until satiated. The remainder of the carcass is covered with debris. After a few days, the lion may return to feed again. A cougar will not eat putrified meat or animals killed by other predators, preferring instead to dine on the fresh meat of its own kills.

While its usual prey is deer, a cougar may kill and eat almost anything edible that crosses its path at the wrong time. Insects, mice, rabbits, bobcats, grouse and elk are all eaten. Surprisingly, most lions autopsied here in Montana by game officials have had porcupine quills imbedded in their forelimbs, indicating that even these formidable rodents may fall prey to the big cats.

While many writers credit lions with choosing sick or weak prey, a study by Maurice Hornacker in neighboring Idaho does not bear this out. He found that any deer or elk spotted in a position where it could be stalked was apt to become dinner. He did note that lions may pass up mature six-point bull elk in favor of smaller individuals. He suspected the lions may have a healthy respect for the massive antlers which are fully capable of injuring or killing the lion.

However, cougars can and do take mature bull elk, and individuals doing so have performed a feat unequaled by any of the other large cats in the world — that of single-handedly dispatching a very tough animal weighing as much as five times its own weight.

With the exception of breeding pairs and females with kittens, cougars are loners. Each individual lives in its own home area and rarely ventures outside that area. Its home area may be as large as 100 square miles but usually includes 20 to 30 square miles.

Home areas of adjacent cougars often overlap to a considerable degree. Even so, meetings between neighbors are rare and fights are almost unheard of. Their solitude is maintained through a mutual avoidance system which uses both visual and chemical means to advertise their presence. Throughout their home area, and often near their kills, cougars make "scrapes" of leaves, dirt, fir or pine needles and mark them with urine or feces. Intruding cats encountering fresh sign detour or otherwise avoid the resident cat.

A female with kittens faced with an intruding male is a notable exception to this pattern of non-aggression. Males have been known to kill and eat unprotected kittens and the female will defend her kittens with tooth and claw.

Females may come in heat year round, but here in Montana breeding most often occurs in winter or early spring. Resident males breed with females that have home areas overlapping their own. Two or three (sometimes as many as five) spotted kittens are born about 90 days later. The den is usually located in a cave, under a rock ledge or beneath a windfall. The kittens are raised on a diet of milk and meat. After they reach about 20 pounds, the kittens leave the birth den and begin to travel with the mother and take refuge in temporary dens while she is hunting. The kittens remain with the female for 18-22 months while they learn to hunt and kill for themselves.

Immediately upon being thrust into independence, the juveniles begin roaming nomadically. They continue to roam until they find a site of sufficient size, with ample resources, and few resident lions. They then settle down to become breeding adults.

*The mountain lion, one of nature's most elusive and seldom seen species.*

a

b

c

d

e

# Lynx and Bobcat

Although the lynx generally is associated with the northern forests and the bobcat with open areas, in Montana there are different areas that accommodate both. Spruce and Douglas-fir communities are home to the lynx, and badlands and foothills are the primary home of the bobcat.

The lynx can be distinguished from the bobcat by its larger size, longer ear tufts, and a black tip on the tail. The tip of the bobcat's tail is black on the upper side only. Typical weights for the bobcat range from 15 to 25 pounds; for the lynx, 15 to 40 pounds.

Although bobcats and lynx have five toes on each front foot and only four on each hind foot, the tracks of both front and rear feet are similar. This is because the fifth toe, corresponding to our thumb, is so high on the inside of the foreleg that it normally does not touch the ground. During normal travel the claws are always in the retracted position and never show in the tracks. All native cats have a tendency to place the hind feet in the tracks left by the front feet, so that in effect each track is a double print. This may be one of the reasons the approach of cats is so silent. In fact the only time they may be heard is during the winter when big toms give vent to murderous howls and screams. The howls are intended to serve as a warning to other toms that they should stay away from their waiting mates.

Like other members of the cat family, bobcats are stealthy hunters, depending upon good eyesight and silence to creep up on their prey. While the lynx is sufficiently dependent on the snowshoe hare to show population fluctuations that correspond with those of its host, the bobcat has a much less discriminating appetite. It too loves snowshoe hares and rabbits, but takes various other animals as opportunity offers. Both species are reliably reported to eat porcupines, young pronghorns, sheep, poultry and game birds. Occasionally one may attempt to kill an adult deer.

Throughout the years both the lynx and bobcat have shifted between the category of predator and fur bearer. In 1966, the Montana legislature chose to ignore the lynx and to categorize it as neither.

Because of the relatively low value placed on the hides of bobcat and lynx, a bounty price was placed on their scalp for many years. It is doubtful that the bounty system is effective in controlling any of the predatory species. Montana, as well as other states, has discovered that vast sums of money are spent without appreciably affecting the population of predators.

a

*Through the years the bobcat (b) and lynx (a) have been the subjects of unlimited hunting and trapping as a predator, then sought under quota as a furbearer. They are not categorized at this time. (c) Bobkitten.*

c

b

# BLACK BEAR

The black bear resembles man more than any other North American mammal, a similarity that becomes startling when the dead creature's enormous fur coat is removed. American Indians noticed this resemblance and they respected this fellow-denizen of the woods, though they hunted it for food and for pelt. But when they killed a bear they apologized for the necessity. They believed its spirit went to the same "Happy Hunting Grounds" as their own, and they courted his good will by putting up strange icons to his memory. Skulls cleaned of flesh were placed at the top of tall poles and their removal was considered taboo.

In addition to a superficial resemblance, the black bear has some of the most engaging of human characteristics. When hungry, it has learned a little acting will bring forth food. Standing on hind legs, it may implore with outstreached paws. Should this entreaty fail, a bear may turn to more direct means and break into cars, cabins, trunks and tents.

In Montana, blacks have clawed and wounded numerous persons. In North America, there are seven cases where blacks have actually become killers. Much of the bear's disrespect for people rests directly on the shoulders of some individuals who have given into the panhandling nature of blacks.

For years the National Park Service tolerated the actions of a misinformed public, believing visitors had an inalienable right to see bears close up. But this is no longer the case, and most of today's bears have been forced to give up hot dogs and potato chips and earn a living on their own.

Under normal circumstances the black bear feeds on most anything, and if any animal on this continent can be said to be totally omnivorous, this bear qualifies. On the vegetable side, it turns readily to grasses and sedges, and in Glacier the authors have seen places where it has torn out great chunks of bark. The inner bark, or cambium layer is quite palatable and exceedingly nutritious.

The list of fruits on its menu includes everything the bear can find: buffaloberries and snowberries, strawberries, cow parsnip, huckleberries and service berries to mention only a few.

Although black bears might prefer meat, they are usually too clumsy to catch a healthy animal, though occasionally they overtake a porcupine.

Garbage, of course, is a bear's haute cuisine. Nothing else is so delectable and there is virtually nothing that can keep him from getting it (see side bar).

a

b

*(a) Because of claws that are considerably shorter and stiffer than those of a grizzly, black bears can readily scurry up a tree.*

*(b) Beggar bears are no longer a common sight in Glacier or Yellowstone National Parks. Strict law enforcement by park service officials has discouraged free handouts. As a result visitors sustain fewer injuries and happily fewer black bears must be sentenced to death.*

Occasionally, a black bear discovers that sheep, goats, calves, or even cattle are helpless victims. One 27-year-old Montana bear killed 24 sheep in a single day. Nearly toothless, it remained fat on its easy prey until it was dispatched.

Black bears enter the world as one of the smallest in relation to the size of their mothers of North American mammals. Only young opossums are smaller, and they are sheltered in a pouch. Two cubs per sow is the typical litter size, though three and occasionally even four cubs per sow is not unusual.

Young blacks are about 9 inches long at birth, weigh 6 to 8 ounces each and are blind, hairless and toothless. Three to four weeks later they open their eyes but do little more than continue suckling. The sow remains oblivious to the squirming bodies and dozes on until ready to emerge from hibernation.

Actually it is a misnomer to say that bears hibernate. Unlike chipmunks, which cannot be aroused because of reduced metabolic processes, the breathing, heartbeat and body temperature of the hibernating bear is not much different from that of a bear snoozing on a hot summer's afternoon. Nor do all bears in North America hibernate. In Montana bears are in winter quarters about the time snow comes, and may remain there for six or seven full months. At the other extreme bears inhabiting the more southerly climes seldom den at all.

Montana bears den about late October, then, about January or February, give birth to their cubs. Several months after the cubs are born the sow and her young leave the den. Cubs now weigh about four pounds and they can walk but are unsteady on their feet. At this stage of their lives they are much better climbers and take to the trees at the first nudge from their mother. If one should dally it is cuffed by the sow and the mistake is not made again.

Cubs remain with their mothers through one summer and until the start of the next. At this time they are about 16 months old, weigh about 50 pounds, have been weaned recently and are capable of foraging for themselves — though the fact needs to be promoted. Helping to drive home the point is a sow whose disposition has suddenly altered. She cuffs the cubs repeatedly and nips at their flanks until it soon becomes abundantly clear to the cubs that they are no longer wanted. At long length, the sow wanders off, watched by cubs who realize they can no longer follow. For a year the cubs may travel together or until they are about two and one-half years old. Then they will disperse, mate briefly and become hermits like their elders.

a

b

Shortly after leaving her cubs, a sow comes into heat and remains in that condition until she encounters a boar. If more than one is encountered, fierce fighting may break out between rival males. Hunters examining bears they have harvested know this from the old scars covering the face and head of their kill. Ears too may have been slashed and appear as nothing more than tattered ribbons.

Clashes between bears, as well as many other animals, are prevented after animals have established a home range. Home range varies in size from area to area and region to region. In the Flathead Valley of northern Montana the size of a black bear's home range is about 12 miles square. Once acquired other bears usually won't infringe upon it. Rather than incur the wrath of an animal having the psychological advantage of being on and defending its own turf, most bears would rather move on and establish areas of their own.

Bears have an uncanny sense of location. Blacks trapped in Glacier and Yellowstone National Parks and relocated frequently return. Many have been moved 30 or more miles; within days they are back.

c

d

(a) Black bears frequently use trees for sharpening their claws or demarcating territory.

(b) In the spring, black bears feed on new growth grass.

(c) Black bear in winter den.

(d). Black bear yearling.

# BEARS IN HEADLINES

*MARAUDING BEAR SENDS CAMPERS HOME From an Associated Press Bulletin, with a Libby, Mont., August 1956 dateline:*

A marauding grizzly drove two men and a horse from the woods in the Minor Lake area about 12 miles east of here.

Al Morton and Del Lucan were on a camping trip and were spending the night on one of the lakes when they heard the bear prowling around the campsite.

Toward morning the two fishermen went out to get their horse and were just in time to see the 11-year-old mare tearing off over the mountain.

The two men walked eight miles back to the Morton ranch. The horse was in the corral, its back torn by the claws of the bear. Morton said the bear must have leaped onto the horse's back.

*From the Helena Weekly Independent 1879: (The setting is a wagon train enroute from Minnesota to the Montana gold fields in 1866.)*

Jo had not succeeded in introducing himself far into the thicket before the bear "rose up immediately before him as big as an elephant," and at the same time made a noise very much like a "frightened hog." Jo, not having the fear of wild beasts before his eyes, instantly fired at the huge animal and commenced backing out of the bushes. The others who were standing back ready to help Jo, now found a difficulty which they had not before thought of. They could not shoot at the bear without standing an equal chance of killing Jo, and Jo was constantly shooting his Henry (rifle). Crack, crack, crack, went Jo's rifle, while he was coolly stepping back . . .

But just then, as ill luck, chance, accident or fortune would have it, one of the cartridges clogged in the breech of the Henry and in an instant that formidable weapon was utterly worthless for present use, except as a club. The bear advanced and closed in upon the poor half-breed who, attempting to defend himself with his "club," became entangled in the brush and fell down, and then the bear was upon him.

Jo gave his hand to the grizzly and, taking the advantage thus gained, thrust his arm directly down his throat, and seized hold and held on with the "grip of death." Pat McGuire (a small-sized wiry built Irishman) rushed to his rescue, came up to Mr. Grizzly and coolly blew off the top of his majesty's head with a Springfield musket while Jo was yet holding onto his tongue.

Jo was somewhat injured but soon recovered, and was able to walk to camp.

*From the JUDITH BASIN STAR, 1922: (The setting is the Slough Creek Ranger Station in Yellowstone National Park in 1922):*

"Ranger Friend was making his first trip of the season to the station," said the assistant district forester. "He rode up to the station on his saddle horse and tied it to a hitch nearby. As Friend stepped onto the porch, he was greeted by a large grizzly bear, who immediately objected to his trespass. Friend shot the animal and, turning, observed another approaching from behind the barn. This was dispatched. Yet another grizzly came from the other side of the house where a pile of tin cans was heaped in a garbage barrel and it met a like fate. When the fourth bear made its appearance, a large yearling, Friend found his gun was empty. Remembering there were some cartridges inside the house on a shelf near the window on the veranda and, breaking the glass, secured a handful of shells and loaded his gun as he went through the sash. The bear in the meantime had changed tactics and running around the house entered at the back door.

Friend sent a bullet through the heart of the bear as he leaped at him across a large kitchen table, placed in the doorway between the kitchen and the living room.

*GRIZZLY FALLS AFTER TEN GUNSHOTS From the BOZEMAN TIMES, June 7, 1877:*

We have received the particulars of an interesting encounter between Mr. Wm. Roe and a large grizzly bear which took place near Virginia Creek. Mr. Roe, having occasion to go to the head of his ditch, took his rifle with him expecting to see some game. There being snow on the ground, he discovered the tracks of a large grizzly bear, following which he soon came upon the animal. Having approached within about one hundred yards of him, Mr. Roe fired, shooting him through the heart. The bear picked himself up and advanced upon Mr. Roe, and when he was within 35 or 40 steps, he raised himself on his hind legs, when he received another bullet in the neck, but he was still too plucky to give up the fight and kept nearing Mr. Roe, receiving, in all, ten shots, the last in his open mouth, when he was only five steps from his antagonist. The bear weighed 732 pounds, after being dressed and having the head, neck, and legs close to his body taken off.

# GRIZZLY BEAR

by Bert Gildart

High on a mountain meadow in the heart of Glacier National Park a humpbacked bear stirred. At first it moved slowly and agilely down a water-carved depression. Then suddenly, with long strides that churned up sod beneath its lethal claws, muscles rippling under its thick, frost-tipped fur, it fled — continuing its flight even after it reached a clump of alpine fir, finally disappearing from sight.

From astride our horses on a slope drenched with lupine, glacier lilies and harebells, we could hear the snapping of twigs as the bear plunged on, still intimidated by its unexpected confrontation with two of its relatively diminutive fellow Earth inhabitants.

Ours was a three-day journey, and during the course of that 1978 summer pack trip, then-Superintendent Phillip Iversen and I had seen five grizzlies. Each of these huge beasts had responded just as do most grizzly bears when they encounter humans — it ran.

But occasionally wilderness wanderers encounter a very different type of bear. And then the public wonders, "What went wrong?" or "What can be done?" In the summer of 1980 two grizzly bears didn't run, and three people were killed.

In the first case, the bodies of Kim Eberly and Jane Ammerman were discovered by two fishermen along a creek bed near a tourist town adjacent to Glacier Park. In the second, the remains of Lawrence Gordon were found at a backcountry campsite where he died alone. The only evidence left of Mr. Gordon was his skull, pelvis and a few other bones. Afterward, instead of just wondering what went wrong, many people responded to the second question, "What can be done?"

"Glacier National Park is attempting to accomplish the impossible," wrote a concerned citizen. "Glacier Park cannot be both a grizzly bear preserve and a heavily used hiking area. You must make a choice to be one or the other." Park managers and most bear biologists do not agree. Guided now by the recommendations of the two boards that gathered information on Glacier's three 1980 deaths, they believe they can strike a compatible balance between Man and bear. But considering the three maulings, it is little wonder the public is growing impatient.

*If you encounter a grizzly in the wild, do not run. This 800 lb. animal can catch an elk.*

Is the National Park Service really doing its job? Can we preserve the national parks for future generations so they will represent our pristine heritage — including the grizzlies — as required by the Congressional mandate of 1916?

I've been an employee of the National Park Service for 13 summers, riding the trails for several of those years as a back country ranger. During that time, I've seen 76 grizzlies, and, with one exception, my encounters stirred awe and admiration for this huge omnivore. But there is that one gruesome exception. In 1967, I helped load the mutilated body of a young woman into a death sack. Later, I returned to shoot the creature as it charged from a distance of 30 feet.

My immediate reaction was one of anger and frustration, similar to that of Lloyd Smith Parratt, an Olympic National Park naturalist who was mauled in 1960 when he was 10 years old. "Why me?" said Smitty. "I didn't do anything." Today, 26 plastic-surgery operations later, Smitty is frank. "Because of my experiences I wouldn't feel comfortable in an area where there are grizzlies — I feel sorry about that — but I don't want to see the bears eliminated in Glacier, either. It's one of the last strongholds of this magnificent creature left in America."

That the grizzly bear represents an integral part of our American heritage is beyond question. American Indians not only learned to co-exist with the grizzly, but they deified it.

With the arrival of the white man, the life of the bear began to change. Early explorers, such as Lewis and Clark, chronicled the activities of the "white bears" on many separate occasions. During their two-year sojourn, members of the expedition killed at least 43, and from that time the grizzly's kingdom began to crumble. Where once it had roamed the plains west of the Mississippi, most were gone by the 1920s.

Most settlers had considered the big bears a scourge interfering with the raising of cattle. Bounties were paid, and they were hunted like vermin. Today, the domain has practically diminished to two of our national parks, Yellowstone and Glacier, and areas surrounding these "reservoirs," where there are maybe 1,000 left, probably fewer. But even in these areas, they are being squeezed from their habitat as a rising number of visitors flock to the parks and inhibit the grizzly's freedom of movement.

The bulk of the North American grizzly population — difficult to count — lives in Alaska and western Canada. Dr. Stephen Herrero, professor of biology and environmental science at the University of Calgary, gives what he calls a seat-of-the-pants estimate: 15,000-20,000 for Canada, and 10,000-15,000 for

*Grizzly cub.*

Alaska. Even in the more remote Denali National Park in Alaska, where the grizzly population is estimated to be about 300, the encounters between people and bears are on the increase and are considered by chief naturalist Bill Truesdell a serious concern. Said Truesdell, "Ten years ago we didn't have that kind of activity, but as we have more visitors, we have the potential for some serious problems. We've had bears approaching people in the back country and raiding camps for food."

Although in the past Indians killed grizzlies for food and clothing and the earlier whites slaughtered them to reduce their numbers, neither produced any radical change in the bear's natural avoidance of Man.

The practice of modifying the grizzly bear's behavior was reserved for inhabitants of more modern times who established garbage dumps and created light-weight backpacking equipment manageable by virtually anyone drawn by the wilderness. The results have been to bring people and bears closer together.

Garbage has had the most profound effect. In 1872, Yellowstone National Park was created and with it began a problem that, years later, would generate the need for a specific Bear Management Plan. The biggest mistake was to permit the creation of garbage dumps. Hotel managers would place garbage adjacent to their establishments to attract wildlife for the amusement of visitors. Records indicate that the hotels had the tacit approval of Yellowstone National Park supervisors and that at least the acting superintendent of 1902 acquiesced in the procedure. Nevertheless, he recognized an incipient danger when he wrote, "Whenever a bear becomes vicious or dangerous at any hotel or station throughout the park, the fact should at once be reported, and a scout will be specifically detailed for the purpose of capturing or killing it."

Perhaps the most famous controversy in the history of wildlife management involved bears and garbage dumps in Yellowstone. Two well-known wildlife researchers, Frank and John Craighead, began a study of the grizzly bears there in 1959. After studying as many as 900 grizzlies over 12 years, they urged the Park Service to phase out dumps slowly, to avoid making the bears marauders that would then have to be shot. The Park Service stuck to its decision to close the dumps cold turkey, and after bitter argument, the Craigheads research was terminated in 1971.

Their approaches were different, but their concern was the same: re-establishment of a wholly wild grizzly population with an all-natural diet, for the sake of both Man and bear.

The first bear-caused death in Yellowstone had been recorded years before, in 1907. A tourist prodded a grizzly cub in a tree with his umbrella; moments later the sow fatally mauled the man. In 1916, a man died after he was dragged off by a grizzly that had been raiding camps for several weeks.

At the time, many authorities felt the killing was out of character for grizzlies. The guilty bear was destroyed, but nothing was done to the garbage dumps, and, by the 1930s, feeding bears the refuse from hotels had become an institution. Bleachers were erected and the bear show become a favorite park attraction drawing people from all over the world.

As the years went by, however, park officials expressed concern that dump grounds would one day constitute a lethal hazard. That "one day" arrived on an August night in 1967.

Sixty years after Yellowstone experienced its first grizzly bear death, Glacier National Park experienced "the impossible." Two young women were killed on the same night in two different valleys. One died near

Granite Park Chalet, where grizzlies were baited with garbage so Chalet guests could get a closer look.

The other incident occured at Trout Lake, a back country campground, exquisite but for the garbage left behind by thoughtless campers. One week after the mauling, Ruben Hart, Glacier's chief ranger during those days, and I returned and gathered 17 burlap sacks of refuse.

Following Glacier's first deaths, both Glacier and Yellowstone implemented plans to separate people and bears — all bears, since the plans cover both grizzlies and black bears. These smaller cousins, which are found in parks in the East as well, may not be as dangerous but they can cause a lot of problems. They're inquisitive, there are more of them and they are apt to become overly familiar with Man, his belongings and his food. "The grizzly is more of a loner," said Glacier National Park management assistant Joe Shellenberger, "and tends to exhibit territorial defensive behavior. The out-and-out attack-type thing that can occur with a grizzly usually doesn't occur with a black bear." But black bears can be a real nuisance, tear up camps or cause injuries to people who cross them. "Tourists try to feed them by hand, or a bear will take a picnic basket and the person will try to take it back and get hurt," he said. "We just had to destroy two black bears that had become too used to people and their food." The evidence against the bears was based on ranger and tourist reports, and one already had been relocated once and tagged as a troublemaker.

Glacier's Bear Management Plan, revised annually, prescribes that anyone who sees a bear report it to a park official, noting the time and location of the sighting, the bear's color and size, and its disposition: aggressive, retiring, fearful, placid, etc. If reports of an aggressive bear begin to accumulate, an investigation is made. The reports also assist biologists in analyzing movements of the bears.

In Glacier these movements vary with the seasons. Sometime in November the grizzlies begin their hibernation in dens located on north- and east-facing slopes at elevations generally above 5,000 feet. In April, they emerge from their dens. Some head for snow-free slopes, others for rivers, places where they expect to find food. They eat grasses and carrion such as goats killed by avalanches. By early June, in mating season, the bears are likely to be moving to remote areas at higher elevations. During the tourist season, in the absence of garbage dumps, they move into subalpine feeding areas and begin to fatten. In the fall, they disperse throughout the park, not confining themselves to any specific location. They feed on buffalo berries, roots and an occasional elk.

*Carrion constitutes a considerable portion of a grizzly's diet.*

Very few visitors ever see a bear, much less encounter one. Because of this they often are incensed by the literature pressed on them. "Why," they ask, "is Glacier trying to scare us to death?" The reply is usually couched in calming phrases, as it should be: "Well, the park is attempting to counter the 'Gentle Ben' syndrome. And then there's this thing called the Federal Tort Claims Act . . ."

That 1964 law allows the public to sue federal agencies. To warn visitors of the hazards, the Bear Management Plan prescribes no fewer than 10 pieces of printed material advising that indeed Glacier is grizzly bear country. Signs depicting vicious bears are everywhere: on outhouse doors, at trail heads, beside roads — little is exempt. Pamphlets, too, are dispensed: one "bear alert" flyer projects from the top of all other literature distributed at entrance gates. Naturalists incorporate information about bears into their lectures.

In general, the information tells you to make noises while hiking, to keep food in closed containers, and to hang food well away from campsites. Women are cautioned not to hike while menstruating. If a bear is encountered, the advice is not to run as that may excite the animal, and a human cannot outrun a grizzly. If a tree is available, and there is time, climb it; otherwise, slowly back away. If the bear attacks assume the fetal position and play dead. Difficult as that sounds, it worked for park ranger Steve Fry who, when he was a teen-ager, was hiking in Glacier and found himself so close to a grizzly that he didn't have time to head for a tree. He dropped immediately next to a log and lay still while the bear sniffed him head to toe. "The situation was so incredible that I hardly had time to think about being terrified," he says.

Rangers like Fry are required by the Bear Management Plan to conduct regular bear patrols in their respective areas. As a back country ranger from June 1 through Labor Day, I do the same, alert for signs of bears — scats, paw prints, and churned up sod, a sign that bears have been digging for roots or small mammals. If I see a sign, I investigate to try to assess the extent of the bear's activities and where it is spending its time. Then, in most instances, I will post the trail head advising hikers of the bear's presence. If I see a bear, I report it to the communications center.

For a number of seasons, I have worked out of a valley near East Glacier Park where once it was necessary for me to close a large portion of the valley to hikers. My log recalls the circumstances:

". . . rode to Pitamakan Pass. Just above Katoya Lake saw a grizzly bear that immediately took flight. Bear was about 350 pounds, black with silver-tipped hair. Continued on down trail and moments after sighting, horse became very nervous, swinging head from side to side trying to look behind. Turned around in saddle and not more than 30 feet behind was grizzly advancing toward us. Stopped horse, grizzly took off but moments later, reappeared. Again I stopped horse and this time the bear departed for good. Horse never bolted. Closed trail later in day. Warm day with little wind."

One week later I reopened the trail, but only after watching the bear for several consecutive days through binoculars as it placidly grazed on grasses and roots across a large lake away from the trail and campground. Several weeks later, the campground was moved down the trail, farther from this prime grizzly bear habitat.

For a number of years the Bear Management Plan appeared to be working. But in 1976 a girl was killed in a car campground in the heart of the populated Many Glacier Valley. That illustrated another problem. Not only does garbage contribute to fatalities, but the inevitable contact bears have with people produces a potentially lethal condition called, in official jargon, habituation. From 1950 to 1980 the number of people visiting the park swelled from 500,000 to more than 1.5 million visitors per year. Compound this increase with the approximately 20,000 who register for permission to use Glacier National Park's back country overnight campsites each summer and the hordes of daytime hikers, and the stage is set to reinforce habituation.

Habituation has long been recognized as a problem confronting parks having garbage, bears and large numbers of visitors. Managers have attempted to alleviate the problem through a process known as aversive conditioning. This concept is designed to reinstill fear

a

b

*(a) Dish pan face, long claws, and frost-tipped fur are characteristics that say, "This one's a grizzly."*

*(b) Grizzly tracks. Note claw marks that extend a full three inches from the pad.*

in bears and is a stated Glacier National Park research objective.

The idea is to employ some stimulus that will condition bears to either refrain from coming to garbage dumps or run at the sight of people. Many possibilities have been tried, so far without success: creosote, electric prods, mace, tear gas and even rock salt fired from shotguns. At Cut Bank Ranger Station, where I have served for several summers, my predecessor tried the last. "Blasted one several times from a distance of 20-30 feet," says Kerel Hagen. "Loud boom associated with some pain. But it never worked. Within half an hour the bear was right back near the campground."

Two of the three people mauled in Glacier National Park last summer were killed by a garbage-habituated bear, similar to those involved in the 1967 deaths.

Though the dump involved, known as the St. Mary dump, was located about one-quarter mile outside the park on the Blackfeet Indian Reservation, it was common knowledge that grizzly bears from the park had been frequenting it.

In the St. Mary area it was well known that bears were creating problems. About a mile outside the park, the Hungry Horse News reported, a bear killed one of Shelbie Woodward's pigs. At St. Mary's townsite, perhaps 100 yards from the park, lodge owner Hugh Black lost a pig to a bear. On July 3, rangers attempted to trap a dark brown grizzly at the dump. The bear also was seen on July 4, but as the board investigating the fatalities of 1980 notes, because the bear "appeared shy of the trap" and because of the busy holiday weekend, the trap was removed.

In previous years, other bears have been seen in the St. Mary area, and in the late '70s, Dr. Charles Jonkel, an internationally recognized authority on bears, tried to have the dump closed. "I tried to emphasize the magnitude of the problem but the park advised me it was out of its jurisdiction," said Jonkel. "At the time, response from the reservation was no better. It was apathetic." The St. Mary dump is now closed, but as of this writing an undetermined number of dumps are still located almost immediately adjacent to the park's boundary.

On July 24, 1980 Kim Eberly and Jane Ammerman had decided to remain overnight in an area not specifically authorized for camping. It was a fatal decision because they were killed by a dark brown grizzly. According to the board of inquiry appointed to consider the incident, the campsite was "on the most logical route for bears moving between the park and garbage sources outside the park." Not surprisingly,

a

b

c

(a) Characteristic hump is discernable near (a) and far (c).

(b) Grizzly bear cache showing attempt to cover elk carcass.

the offending bear was later shot in the same area.

The board also provides further comments regarding the couple's camping:

"Had they indicated an intent to camp in the St. Mary area in other than one of the designated campgrounds, it is likely they would have been informed that a grizzly bear had been visiting the (St. Mary) dump . . . Had Mr. Eberly and Ms. Ammerman been responsive to information received during their orientation (they were both concession employees) and adhered to park regulations, they would not have been killed."

Eberly and Ammerman were camped on a sandbar in the middle of a small creek less than 6 feet wide. Pushing through a clump of willows on a warm spring day, I found the spot. In spring the tourists were gone, but, still, I could hear the occasional roar of a vehicle as it hummed along the nearby highway. Occasionally, muted voices could be heard.

About half a mile away was a now-deserted campground. A short distance in the other direction was the tourist town of St. Mary. Time slipped by as the warm sun engulfed me and for a moment I was mesmerized by drips from the exhausted winter creek. But this was early spring and the sudden flutter of a bird taking wing gave me a start. Thirteen years ago, three other men and I had found the mutilated body of Michele Koons on just such a day when birds sang and life seemed to surge.

In the second 1980 incident, circumstances were different. The bear believed to have killed Lawrence Gordon had a history of aggressiveness. It had been trapped in 1978 and moved from the populated Many Glacier Valley over the Continental Divide to Valentine Creek, a distance of about 30 miles. In 1980, according to park biologist Cliff Martinka, the bear returned to Many Glacier Valley. On either September 26 or 27, it killed Lawrence Gordon at nearby Elizabeth Lake.

Following the Gordon death, another board convened. This one advised Glacier to reevaluate what constitutes a problem bear. Previously, overtly aggressive behavior was necessary before a bear was considered a problem. This board suggested that the park take a harder line on any bear that has torn up camps, eaten other than natural food, or simply become overly familiar with humans. The board advised that such bears should be trapped and immediately removed — either transplanted or killed.

The board also suggested that the availability of natural food for the grizzlies should be evaluated periodically. This belief is predicated on the assumption that bears tend to be more troublesome when food stress exists. Expert Charles Jonkel adds that the condition of bears should also be assessed. This information can be gathered from the animals tranquilized by rangers and researchers. No Monday-morning quarterback, Jonkel warned on radio, prior to the discovery of Gordon's death, that conditions existing in northwestern Montana were volatile. He argued, "When food

is scarce and the condition of bears is poor, these animals begin to wander and seek out new areas having adequate sustenance. During these times Glacier authorities should manage their domain by excluding people from certain areas."

The Gordon board also believed that the transplant program could be improved. If it were necessary to capture a bear, the board said, it probably would be "troublesome enough (for us) to seriously question if it should be transplanted within the park." Preferably, other agencies should take the bear; if this is not possible, the bear should be destroyed. This advice was given with knowledge that Glacier National Park's grizzly bear population of about 200 appears to be stable.

This stability is a very tenuous thing. Grizzly bears have one of the lowest reproduction rates of any mammal in North America. During the course of a lifetime, a grizzly female gives birth to from six to 10 cubs on the average, and many of these will not live to adulthood. For these reasons, bear managers are reluctant to shoot a grizzly.

Since 1967 the park has killed 15 bears for management purposes, slightly more than one a year. This year, things may change. At least that's what the new, improved, 1981 Bear Management Plan says, for the park has accepted all but one of the recommendations made by the Ammerman-Eberly and Gordon review boards. The one exception is that the park will not insist (although it will suggest) that backpackers be accompanied by other hikers. Gordon had been a lone hiker.

All other recommendations are now an integral part of the 1981 Bear Management Plan. The park is taking an active role on garbage disposal sites in areas adjacent to government land. It is beginning to monitor the availability of the natural food of the grizzlies and their general condition. During times when the bears are under stress, the Park is prepared to exclude people from specific areas. The Bear Management Plan accepts that, in certain circumstances, troublesome bears should be killed.

Will this plan absolutely separate humans and grizzlies? No. But then, where do we find any such guarantees? Certainly not in Glacier, where grizzlies have contributed to six of the park's 150 deaths from its opening in 1910 through the Gordon death last September.

If the public considers this fraction an unacceptably large number and insists on access to every last one of Glacier's valleys, then the only alternatives left are to construct huge hurricane-type fences around back-country campsites, provide armed escort service for the public — or totally eliminate the grizzly.

For one who thrives on freedom and firmly believes that the original Congressional mandate of 1916 should be preserved, none of these solutions would be acceptable. Instead, I believe we should be willing to accept the continued improvements in a plan that can provide a good probability of increased protection. Now all the plan needs is proper implementation and a compassionate public — one willing to give this creation of the ages a brief reprieve.

But for the grizzly bear it is very, very late in the day. I remember once when I encountered a pair of littermates near Glacier's Surprise Pass. Twilight was creeping in along the trail and moments earlier an elk had bugled into the crisp September air. A leaf swirled to the ground and just as silently, two grizzlies rounded a nearby bend in the trail. An evening zephyr stirred and carried with it some secret message. Sensing intrusion, one of the bears rose on its hind feet, the other followed suit.

Instinctively, I stood. With incredible speed the bears dropped to all fours and whirled. Muscles rippled, sod churned, branches whisked. Run, I thought, run before you are lost.

*Many biologists consider the grizzly to be an indicator of the quality of wilderness. "When the grizzly is gone," they say, "so too will be the wilderness."*

# MINK

The wild mink, the original source of the more fashionable coats, is a solitary and aggressive animal that looks like a large weasel. Characteristically, mature specimens are about two feet long, dark brown, and sport a small patch — or patches — of white on the chin, throat, or chest.

Because of their lightning reflexes, mink are excellent predators, although they occasionally fall prey to larger animals such as the lynx, hawk or coyote. Mink are at home both on land and in water, searching for mice, birds, frogs and fish. Muskrats, however, remain their favorite food and, once one of these rodents is disposed of, the mink may move into the muskrat's well-constructed lodge to raise its own young.

Because mink and muskrats are usually co-occupants of lakes, ponds, marshes and rivers, they have been a source of concern to biologists who manage fur bearers. Each species attains a prime pelt at a different season — mink in the fall and muskrat in spring. But as long as the trapping pressure does not increase to the point where populations of spring-captured mink taken in muskrat traps are substantially diminished, the spring muskrat season will continue.

# WEASELS

All three of North America's weasels are found in Montana. The short-tailed weasel is limited to the western half of Montana while the long-tailed weasel is common over the whole state. The least weasel is a rare inhabitant in the eastern half of the state.

As predators, weasels are well equipped for their way of life. With streamlined bodies and small heads, they are adept at squeezing through small places, and with needle-sharp teeth, are effective predators. Like other members of their family, they possess a foul musk gland, but unlike the skunk, are not able to spray.

Weasels eat about a third of their weight every 24 hours and include in their diet such animals as shrews and mice. Weasels have few enemies, but sometimes one may meet its match when it attacks a large snake.

Weasels move in graceful bounding leaps and their characteristic twin prints are a common sight in the winter snow.

*a*

(a) Mink.

(b) In winter, weasels are known as ermine.

(c) Short-tailed weasel.

*b*

*c*

90

*a*

*River otter antics.*

*b*

*c*

*d*

# Skunk

Less than a mile from the West Glacier visitor center, a park naturalist encountered an enraged skunk. At first, the animal attempted to retreat to the sanctuary of a crevice. As the hole was too shallow to conceal it, it attempted to intimidate its adversary. Upon emerging from the shallow hole, the skunk first stamped its feet, then it again retreated to the crevice. Eight times the skunk retreated only to re-emerge, stamp its feet, arch its back and snap up its tail. The naturalist maintained what she thought to be a safe distance, watching until finally the skunk elevated its hind quarters and poised as though to take aim and fire. Wisely the lady retreated.

Montana's skunks are famous for their remarkable aim. Though prone to discharge their scent only as a last resort, spray they will under duress.

The spray of a skunk is discharged by the contraction of powerful hip muscles on glands located on either side of the anus. The contents of these glands are emitted through two grape-size ducts also located near the anus. The two fine streams of thick, oily, yellowish liquid unite about a foot away into one stream of increasingly fine droplets. This spray is astonishingly accurate up to about 12 feet from the animal. Intruders will usually be struck with a blinding stinging stream. Chemists know the skunk's secretion as N-butyl mercapton sulphur. The sulphur helps give the fluid its evil odor and can cause convulsions and loss of consciousness if a relatively weak animal is sprayed. On damp nights the aroma hangs for weeks, like an invisible mist, to remind all who pass that here someone or some animal made the mistake of challenging a skunk.

Several misconceptions surround skunks. One of these is the idea that you might be safe if (somehow) a skunk can be elevated off the ground by the tail. The idea is to reduce the driving action of the feet, but don't count on it, this kind of a lift doesn't help. The theory has been explored too often.

Another misconception is the belief that if sprayed in the eyes, blindness will result. This is not true. The discharge will cause burning and bring forth a copious flow of tears, but sight will return usually within an hour. Washing the eyes with water may speed the process.

Skin is another problem. Water won't touch the oily residue on the skin unless ammonia or preferably a less volatile petroleum-based product is added. Gasoline on a wash cloth helps, but many consider the best

91

a

b

c

d

*(a) Striped skunk photographed in the Flathead Valley as it searches for a beetle, grub or perhaps a small rodent.*

solvent to be tomato juice. However, whatever treatment is used, it is recommended that the cure be administered out-of-doors. Bathrooms will smell for months if the victimized person or house pet is cleaned inside.

Two skunks, the striped and spotted, are indigenous to Montana, though only the striped is abundant. Of the two, the striped skunk is also more conspicuous, because of its size. Weighing six to 10 pounds and reaching lengths of about two feet, it is one of the several species of skunks found in the United States. At half its cohabitant's size, the spotted skunk is the smallest of those in North America. Their respective names provide the clues for differentiation: Striped skunks have a white stripe which begins at the forehead, divides near the shoulder, and runs along the sides, and terminates at the base of the tail. Spotted skunks have four broken white stripes along the neck, back and sides, some say the spray of a spotted skunk is more potent than that of the striped, though verification of this notion seems to be a test few would be willing to conduct.

Skunks often are denounced for killing ground-nesting birds and, in the past, they have been classified as a predatory species — an animal to be killed on sight. But whatever the skunk's affinity for these winged species, critics should keep in mind that they have saved other birds — namely ducks — by digging up and eating the eggs of snapping turtles.

Skunks include in their diet such things as snakes, lizards, grasshoppers, crayfish, beetles, grubs, small rodents, carrion, and eggs from hen houses. Because of

this later predilection, they are considered pests by local ranchers.

Most animals will not attack a skunk though the great horned owl is a notable exception, and skunks are frequently killed by cars.

Skunks can be seen in virtually all of Montana's ecosystems. The striped skunk ranges throughout the state, frequenting elevations ranging from the lowest to the highest. The spotted skunk, on the other hand, confines itself to the semi-desert habitat of southern Montana. Both species can be found during any of the four seasons though they may retreat to their dens if the weather becomes particularly severe. No skunk is a true hibernator, though some take very long winter naps. A warm spell in mid-winter will mean skunk tracks in the snow.

Sometime in late winter, skunks mate. Following a gestation period of about 60 days, they give birth to their young in a dry, vegetation-lined den underground or in a hollow log, niche, cranny or cave. Litter size varies from two to six. At birth, the young are nearly devoid of fur, their eyes are closed and they weigh less than an ounce. Within a month, they can see and have acquired their fur. Within two months, they are weaned and within four months, they have attained full growth.

Skunks are referred to by names other than "spotted" or "striped." Some call them civet cats while others use the terms phoby cats or hydrophobia cats. The last two terms are derived from the fact that many carry rabies, though they are no more susceptible to rabies than are other animals.

*(b) Raccoons are relative newcomers to Montana.*

*(c) Growler, grunter and hisser — even large predators are reluctant to tackle a badger.*

*(d) Badger near Grass Range.*

92

a

b

*(a) Occasional sightings of the fisher occur in areas surrounding the Flathead Valley.*

*(b) Pine marten*

# WOLVERINE

Wolverines are mostly scavengers but can prey on animals larger than themselves — more than one young moose and elk calf has fallen to this the largest member of the weasel family. Powerful, they may weight 20 to 50 pounds and measure 20 to 30 inches in length. The light, soft fur is covered with long coarse overhairs. Yellow bands are found on the sides and rump of the otherwise dark brown animal.

Because of its rapacious nature it has earned itself several nicknames. Often referred to as glutton, Indian Devil, and wolf marten, the wolverine has the reputation of being the greatest trouble maker in the animal world. A pair of them will destroy a camp or the interior of a cabin. As trap robbers, they have no equal.

# FISHER

The derivation of this weasel's name is unknown, for it isn't particularly fond of fish. Rather, it includes in its diet hares, many different kinds of rodents, and some plants. Fishers are excellent tree climbers and can easily catch red squirrels and even an occasional marten. Fishers are also one of the few successful predators of porcupines.

Fishers disappeared from Montana in the late 1920s and were not seen again until 1959 when 36 were transplanted from areas in British Columbia to Montana. Three areas were selected as transplant sites to include areas near Rexford, Holland Lake in the Swan Valley, and the Rock Creek drainage east of Missoula. Several of the transplanted animals moved a considerable distance, but the longest move was made by a male that traveled approximately 80 air miles from Holland Lake to the town of Creston.

# PINE MARTEN

The marten looks like a large dark brown weasel, but with orange spots on the throat and chest. It is an expert at climbing trees, where it seeks one of its favorite foods, red squirrels. Other prey include pikas, hares, birds and many kinds of rodents. Occasionally, martens may eat a small amount of vegetation.

The lustrous fur of the marten always has been in demand, and, because of its value, these mammals were once heavily trapped throughout the state.

During the 1940s martens were considered Montana's most valuable fur-bearing animal. In the '50s, research was conducted in Glacier National Park to determine if the park served as a reservoir for out-lying areas. Tagging, however, indicated few marten travel far enough to aid populations in adjacent areas. Despite the former trapping, martens are fairly common and today occupy many areas in Montana's mountain ranges.

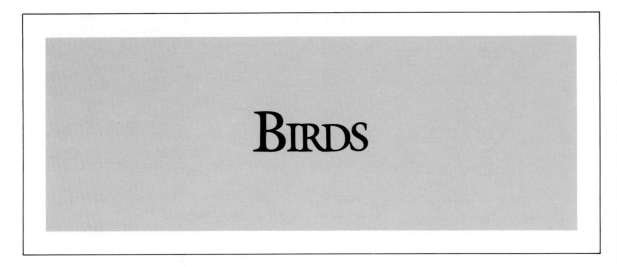

# BIRDS

Mention the word wildlife, and invariably talk turns to the majestic elk, the wary whitetail, the fleet pronghorn and the awe inspiring grizzly. Rarely does the conversation turn to birds — in spite of the fact that there are twice as many different species of birds in Montana than there are mammals, that birds are more readily observed than mammals, and the fact that birds are much more colorful and more vocal than mammals.

Perhaps the reason for this quirk is because relatively few birds are hunted. Or, perhaps it is because birds are everywhere and have become commonplace.

Whatever the reasons, Montanans who watch birds are guaranteed many hours of pleasure and entertainment, as the state is blessed with 378 different species of birds. Of these, 335 have been substantiated by specimens or photographs. While many of these species are migrants that only pass through the state on their way north or south, about 250 species nest here, and many are year-round residents.

The smallest bird in Montana is the calliope hummingbird which measures a mere 2¾ inches in length and weighs about 1/10th of an ounce. The largest bird in Montana is the trumpeter swan which measures about 6 feet in length, has a wingspan of about 8 feet and may weigh as much as 40 pounds.

We have birds of almost any size, shape and color. In addition to different physical characteristics, birds vary widely in their habits, diet, behavior and their ability to sing.

No matter what their form or habit, birds have an abundant supply of beauty, grace and charm which makes them impossible to ignore.

## WILDFOWL

Wildfowl mean different things to different people. To some, they are silent, wavering Vs in the spring sky. To others they are haunting cries in the night or bright splashes of color in spring puddles. To hunters and naturalists, they may be the whistle of wings in the predawn cold, the explosion of wings and water on a secluded oxbow, or a flock of greenheads sideslipping into a spread of decoys. To gourmets, they are an epicurean delight.

Whatever wildfowl mean to you, Montana is endowed with an abundance of them. Of the 35 species of wildfowl that can be seen in the state, three are swans, five are geese, three are mergansers and 24 are ducks. Twenty-three species nest here, and the remaining 12 can be seen only when passing through the state in the spring and fall.

Hunting season length and framework for wildfowl are set by the federal government under treaties with Mexico and Canada. Our state wildlife department sets the opening and closing dates within the federal guidelines. Seasons are set on the basis of continent-wide population figures and do not correlate directly with the available habitat here in Montana. Many of the birds we hunt here in the fall were raised in Canada. Montana includes parts of two flyways, the Central and the Pacific, within its borders. Consequently, regulations east and west of the Divide may vary.

The future of wildfowl in Montana appears bright in spite of the loss of habitat to drainage and various other types of development. This loss is somewhat offset by the creation of stock ponds in the northeastern part of the state. Because of the huge areas of habitat and the relatively few hunters in the state, Montana contributes more birds to the continental population than it harvests. If the needs of waterfowl are considered in future developments, and in the creation of stock ponds and other water projects, biologists believe we may actually be able to increase the production of waterfowl in the state.

## SWANS

Because of their pure white plumage and large size, swans are by far the most impressive of our wildfowl. Two species, the trumpeter swan and the whistling swan, are native to Montana while the third species, the mute swan, has been introduced to limited areas in the southwestern part of the state.

While the mute swan is readily recognized by its orange bill, the other two swans are not so readily identified. Whistlers sometimes have a yellow spot on their bills, while the bills of trumpeters often have a red commisure. Differences in size, although real, are difficult to apply in the field because of the overlap with different-age birds. Biologists who have observed

a

b

c

d

e

f

both species for extended periods of time from close range indicate that there is no sure way, short of hearing them call, to tell the two species apart. The call of the whistler is a weak, high-pitched, wavering call while the call of the trumpeter is deep and resonant with a French horn quality.

Another factor that might help distinguish the two species is the month observations are made. While the trumpeter is a year-round resident in the state, whistlers only pause here on their spring and fall travels.

# GEESE

Of Montana's five species of geese, only the Canada goose is a resident. The snow goose, white-fronted goose, Ross' goose and the brant are migrants. The snow goose occurs in incredible numbers during the spring and fall migrations. Between 300,000 and 400,000 of these white birds with black wingtips use a narrow corridor along the east slope of the Rockies in their travels. Occasionally, a few do stray into the Flathead area.

Traditionally, Canada geese nested only along the river bottoms of the Missouri, Yellowstone and Flathead river systems. There they selected islands, cliffs, abandoned osprey nests and isolated shorelines to build their nests. However, with the building of large dams and the many small stock ponds in the northeast

and other areas of the state, the nesting Canada geese have expanded their range to include those areas. This expansion was helped to some degree by transplant programs that moved geese from the Bowdoin National Wildlife Refuge to Medicine Lake National Wildlife Range, Freezeout Lake, and to the Tongue River near Miles City. In the Hi-Line area, virtually any pond of more than five acres that has a suitable nesting island or peninsula has a pair of nesting Canadas.

*Opposite Page: Whistling swan. This Page (a) Trumpeter swan.*

*(b) Snow geese*

*(c) Canada goose.*

*(d) Goose nest with clutch of five eggs.*

*(e) Gosling.*

*(f) Canada goose.*

*(g) Canada geese with young.*

g

95

# TRUMPETER

The trumpeter was once very plentiful in North America. Between 1853 and 1877, the Hudson Bay Company handled more than 17,000 swanskins, a good portion of them trumpeters. Skins were sold at London markets for adornments and for use in powder puffs and down garments. By 1900 the trumpeter was nearly extinct. Prominent ornithologist, Edward Howe Forbush, wrote in 1912, "total extinction (of the trumpeter) is now only a matter of time." Even so, nothing was done until 1918 when the hunting of trumpeters was outlawed by the Migratory Bird Treaty Act. But then it was almost too late. By 1933, only 69 of these great birds existed in the lower 48 states although there were vague reports of trumpeter populations in Alaska.

The remaining 69 birds all were contained in the Yellowstone-Red Rock Lakes-Jackson Hole region of southwest Montana, northeast Idaho and northwest Wyoming. The purchase of the Red Rock Lakes National Wildlife Refuge by the U.S. Government in 1935 was the first step in the protection of the prime breeding habitat of these birds. The number of birds in the Red Rock Lakes area and the surrounding region increased until the 1950s when the fall counts leveled off at about 600 birds.

As with other animal populations, once the trumpeters had reached the capacity of the range to provide food and cover, other internal mechanisms took control and limited the growth of the population. This was evident by the fact that over half of the cygnets were dying before reaching flight stage in September. This led biologists to try transplanting surplus cygnets to other areas of suitable habitat in the hope of establishing other viable trumpeter populations.

In 1958, the first brood of trumpeters was spotted on the Malheur National Wildlife Refuge in Oregon during a routine waterfowl census. Those cygnets were the progeny of two birds from a group of 20 young swans that had been transplanted from Red Rock Lakes in 1955. Through that transplant it was learned that trumpeters can breed in their third year of life rather than the fourth year as had been previously thought. Since that first successful introduction, trumpeters have been introduced to suitable habitats in Nevada, South Dakota, Washington and Minnesota — many from Montana's Red Rock Lakes.

*a*

*b*

*(a) Trumpeter swan.*
*(b) Trumpeters with young.*

# DUCKS

Of the 24 species of ducks that have been recorded in the state, 18 of them are known to nest here. Although the habitat required by the different species varies to a considerable degree, they all require close proximity to water to raise their broods.

Relatively few ducks winter here, although there are always a few hardy mallards or goldeneye toughing it out in areas of open water. Most other ducks are long gone by the time potholes ice over.

Ducks can be divided into two groups by their structure and their habits. The dabbling or puddle ducks are primarily ducks of shallow waters. As their name implies, they can often be found in shallow pools and roadside puddles where they feed by tipping. When startled, they take flight by jumping directly into the air. This group includes such species as the mallard, pintail, shoveler, gadwall, wigeon, and Montana's three species of teal.

In contrast, the diving ducks are inhabitants of deeper water. They feed by diving, often to great depths. When surprised, they must spring across the surface of the water for several feet to gain the momentum needed to sustain flight. Canvasbacks, redheads, lesser and greater scaup, bufflehead, ruddy ducks and goldeneye are examples of diving ducks.

# WOOD DUCKS

Although more comon to the eastern United States, wood ducks are found nesting in Montana. They prefer woodland areas near water and often nest in abandoned squirrel holes or cavities hollowed by woodpeckers. Near Libby, Montana, a number of bird enthusiasts traditionally build bird houses specifically for wood ducks. View the iridescent beauty of this exquisite bird and it is easy to see why. Another glance and there is no question that there was sufficient justification for honoring the bird three times on stamps. In 1943, and again in 1974, its picture appeared on the Migratory Bird Hunting stamp. In 1968 it was minted as a U.S. postage stamp.

Early in the 20th century, it was feared the wood duck was headed for extinction. Habitat alteration and commercial gunners took a heavy toll. In 1918, the wood duck was placed under protection and today, the bird not only nests, but migrates through both of Montana's flyways.

(a) Male mallard.
(b) Female mallard.
(c) Blue-winged teal.
(d) Male wood ducks.
(e) Male canvasback.
(f) Male Barrow's goldeneye.
(g) Mallard feeding.
(h) Male harlequin duck.
(i) Male northern pintail.
(j) Male and female redheads.
(k) Female scaup.
(l) Male and female hooded mergansers.

# HARLEQUIN DUCK

Most of the ducks of Montana are associated with the relatively calm water of lakes, ponds, marshes and slow moving rivers. Not so the harlequin. It prefers the cold swift waters of mountain streams.

Harlequins, the only sea ducks found in the state, spend their winters along the Pacific coast, diving through the breakers for crustaceans and mollusks. With the coming of spring they move inland to breed, some of them coming as far east as western Montana. Here they seek out the upper reaches of fast, turbulent, icy-cold mountain streams formed by melting snow and ice. They feed by diving and walking on the bottoms of these streams, searching for the larvae of stone and caddis flies.

The lords and ladies, as the males and females are called, conduct a whirlwind courtship. The lady searches out a suitable stump or cavity in the rocks in which to lay her six or seven buffy eggs. As soon as incubation begins, the lord abandons the lady and flies back to the coast where he joins other bachelor lords.

97

a

# WATERBIRDS

Cormorants, grebes, loons, pelicans, herons, egrets, ibises, bitterns, shorebirds, gulls and terns are birds that depend on water to survive. Some, such as the cormorants, grebes and loons, spend almost their entire lives on the water, venturing onto land only to nest and raise their young. With dense bodies, webbed or lobed feet, and legs set well back on their bodies, they swim and dive with ease. But, these same features make them virtually helpless on land.

Facilitated by streamlined bodies, these birds are capable of executing the underwater maneuvers necessary to capture the small fish they eat. Able to dive in a flash, grebes are also capable of sinking slowly out of sight, like miniature submarines.

Not designed for diving, white pelicans feed while floating buoyantly on the water. Unwary fish are captured in the pouch along with several gallons of water. Only after the water has drained, is the fish swallowed.

Although they usually feed alone, pelicans sometimes cooperate while fishing. Ungainly pelicans appear as unlikely participants in an exhibition resembling a well rehearsed water ballet. The show begins with a group of the large birds swimming in a tight U-formation. In unison, they stretch their necks, submerge their heads, tip completely on end like giant puddle ducks, emerge and swim on to repeat the performance a few yards distant.

Another group of waterbirds, more commonly referred to as waders, depends on the water just as much as the previous group of birds. Yet, they seldom do more than get their feet wet. All are tall and slender with long necks, long legs and long bills. Examples are the herons, egrets, ibis and bittern.

In contrast to the webbed feet of the swimming water birds, waders have long toes which prevent them from sinking in soft, mucky, bottom ooze. Some feed by waiting in ambush, others by stalking the shallows and still others by probing the mud. Fish, frogs, snakes, crustaceans and aquatic insects are taken by various members of the group.

Shorebirds also depend on water, or, more particularly, the shoreline. Included in the group are the American avocet, the black-necked stilt, the killdeer, and a large number of small, nondescript, brownish species of birds such as the sandpiper.

Aptly named, the shorebirds patrol the shorelines of lakes, ponds, rivers and streams in search of aquatic insects and other small invertebrates. Shorter than the waders, they hunt either on the beach or in very shallow water, rarely more than inches deep.

Another group of birds commonly associated with water is the family *Laridae* — the gulls and terns. Of the two, gulls are more common. Their heavy bills are hooked at the tip, enabling them to eat almost anything. Virtually any supply of easy food will have its complement of gulls. Look for them feasting in freshly plowed fields, flooded fields, sanitary landfills, nesting colonies of other birds and even supermarket parking lots. Where men do not provide easy food, gulls feed by flying over the water in search of dead or dying fish. They also patrol shorelines searching for grasshoppers and crickets.

In contrast to the gulls, terns are more delicate. Careful observers will notice their thin, pointed bills, narrow wings and forked tails. They fly gracefully over the water in search of small fish, which they capture with a plunging headfirst dive. Rarely do they light on water, preferring, instead, to rest on shore or debris.

b

c

d

*(a) Incubation of the two eggs produced by a pair of pelicans is shared equally.*

*(b) Montana contains two of the 15 pelican rookeries found in the United States. One is located at Medicine Lake, the other at Bowdoin Refuge. Cormorants (c) and California gulls (d) share the nesting areas. Gulls are active predators of pelican eggs.*

*(a) Greater yellowlegs.*

*(b) Least sandpiper.*

*(c) Forster's tern.*

*(d) Black-necked stilt.*

*(e) Snowy egret.*

*(f) American bittern.*

# GREAT BLUE HERON

"He had taken a silent step, and with great care he advances; slowly does he raise his head from his shoulders, and now, what a sudden start! His formidable bill had transfixed a perch, which he beats to death on the ground. See with what difficulty he gulps it down his capacious throat!"

The bird so aptly described above by Audubon is the great blue heron. The heron hunts not only by stalking but also by waiting — motionless, minute after minute — for an unsuspecting fish, frog, snake, crustacean, or almost any other creature small enough to swallow. However, his favorite food is fish and he takes as many as he can skewer.

Try to approach this extremely wary bird and it will rise heavily into the air, neck extended and long gangly legs swinging in time to its wing beats. Once airborne, he folds his neck back in a graceful curve and flies low over the marsh with steady, deliberate strokes of its powerful wings. It glides for a second, extends its legs forward and settles back down in the water with barely a ripple.

Mostly solitary except during the mating season, great blue herons converge on Montana in early spring and congregate at their rookeries. The trees or small islands they choose for their nesting colonies soon are filled with strutting, pecking, croaking and nibbling birds. The male brings sticks to the female which she fashions into the flimsy nest, which will hold her four eggs. Parents take turns incubating until the squabs hatch and then they both help feed their noisy youngsters. Mortality among young herons is high but once they survive their first year, they are very long lived — sometimes 15 to 20 years.

As with many species of wildlife, man appears to be their worst enemy. Draining marshes and eliminating their nesting colonies are the greatest threat to this striking bird.

*(g) Great blue heron.*

*(i) Great blue heron young.*

*(h) Heron shading young.*

a

c

d

e

b

f

(a) American coot and young.

(b) Sandhill crane.

(c) Western grebe.

(d) Red-necked grebe.

(e) Eared grebe.

(f) White-faced ibis.

# WESTERN GREBE

With throats swollen, heads low, crests erect and red eyes bulging, two birds swim slowly toward each other. Quietly they dip their beaks into the water, raise their heads and vigorously shake them from side to side while each makes a rapid clicking sound. Then, as if on signal, they turn sideways, raise upright, arch their wings and necks back in graceful curves. Suddenly, they dash ahead, almost running over the surface of the water. Moments later the pair dives, only to emerge seconds later in unison where they swim calmly, side by side — mating now complete.

This beautifully synchronized performance can be seen every spring after the stately western grebe returns from points south to many of the large marshes in Montana that have an abundance of reeds. Nest building also is performed in unison with both birds contributing to the construction of the floating nest. The male brings the material and the female arranges it.

The pair also shares in the incubation of the three or four bluish eggs. Incubation begins before the second egg is laid, so the young hatch on successive days. After hatching, the pale gray young often ride "piggyback" on the adult birds. They ride just under the wing coverts with only their downy heads sticking out, content to let the adults do the paddling.

# WHITE-FACED IBIS

The white-faced ibis is a relatively rare bird in Montana. Although it has been seen in many different parts of the state, it is observed most frequently at Bowdoin NWR and Benton Lake NWR, where it breeds.

Ibis nest in colonies, often in association with herons, egrets or gulls. The nest itself is built in tall reeds, on floating vegetation or on small islands. It is built from dead reeds and twigs and lined with grass. Both parents incubate the three to four pale blue eggs. Three weeks later the dull-black, downy young hatch. The young grow rapidly on their diet of regurgitated food.

While many of the waders feed by waiting in ambush, the white-faced ibis is a stalker. Moving slowly through the shallow marshes, it probes for food items with its long bill. Insects, small fish, small frogs, tadpoles, invertebrates and earthworms are all eagerly sought.

# WILSON'S PHALAROPE

Unlike most birds, the female Wilson's phalarope is the larger and more colorful of the pair. In summer, the female has a more pronounced neck stripe than the male (pictured) and has a light gray back interspersed with a couple of brown stripes. In fall, the colors of both sexes meld into a pale bluish-gray that characterizes winter plumage.

Role reversal in the phalaropes does not end with plumage. During the breeding season, the female pursues the male. Although he tries to escape, she usually corners him. Even then, the work has just begun for the male. He will line a depression with grass to form a nest. After the female lays the four dark spotted buffy eggs, he will incubate them. And, after the young hatch, he will watch them.

Although phalaropes do feed in the conventional hunt-and-peck manner of other shorebirds, they also have a rather unique feeding method. At times, they can be seen whirling in circles on the surface of the water. The spinning motion creates a vortex that stirs up the bottom muck and carries insect larvae to the surface where they can pick them up without even wetting their heads.

a

c     d

e     f

*(a) Wilson's phalarope.*
*(b) American avocet*

*(c, d, e, f) Killdeer feigns broken wing to lure predators away from young hidden nearby.*

*(g) Willet.*

*(h) Common snipe.*

# AMERICAN AVOCET

The "wheet," "wheet," "wheet" of the American avocet can be heard throughout Montana marshes from early spring to late fall. It is one of the largest and most striking of the shorebirds in the state and frequently can be seen striding across mudflats, wading in shallow water, or resting along shore on one thin leg.

In spring and early summer, the avocet's bold black and white pattern is set off by its long blue legs and its orangish-tan head and neck. Late summer and fall finds the orangish-tan fading into the pale-gray of the avocet's winter plumage before the migration to California for warmer weather.

Avocets frequently can be seen in shallow water making side-to-side sweeps through the bottom ooze with their long, thin, upturned bills. These sweeps disturb the small aquatic animals and insects that the avocets eat.

A shallow depression in the sand or a small platform of grass near water is all the nest necessary for the three or four blotched olive eggs. Almost immediately after hatching, the young leave the nest and head for water. When disturbed, young avocets scurry for cover while the adult birds use a broken-wing ploy to distract the intruder.

b

g

h

# RAPTORS

Raptors are predators that must kill other animals in order to survive. That fact stirs up strong emotions in people and may be the reason these fierce looking birds are often hated. Driving back-country roads, it is not unusual to find an eagle, hawk or owl draped over a barbed wire fence. Had the marksman who shot such a bird understood the amazing skills these birds possess, their disdain almost surely would have been replaced with admiration.

As hunters, raptors are superbly equipped. Their eyes, large in relation to their body size, are believed to have four to eight times the resolving power of our own, enabling the raptors to see things at incredible distances. Peregrine falcons, for example, are reported to have the ability to spot a sitting dove from a distance of 3,000 feet. A rabbit scampering through the grass can be detected by an eagle two miles away. And osprey are capable of distinguishing a neutral colored fish, underwater, from a height of 300 feet.

Positioned to enable the birds to see better while pursuing and striking prey, the eyes are set on the sides and to the front of the head. Should the birds crash through brush while in hot pursuit, their eyes are protected by bony shields projecting over the eyes.

Once spotted, the prey is overtaken by a pursuer plummeting from the sky at blinding speeds, conditions that would blur human vision. Special muscles in their eyes control lens curvature, providing accurate perception of moving objects throughout the dive. Presented with special problems by the refraction of light from water, the fish eaters, such as the bald eagle and the osprey, have visual correction that allows for the double image. Thus, they know the exact location of the fish. Not surprising then, that the eyesight of raptors is said to be the keenest of any living creature.

While their superb eyes are keeping the prey in sight, their legs are preparing for the kill. When the legs are extended, tendons spread the toes which are equipped with powerful claws. At the moment of impact, the legs buckle, automatically closing the talons which pierce the vital organs of the prey. Death is instantaneous.

The powerful hooked beak is then put into service, tearing off bite-sized pieces for consumption.

The raptors in Montana are placed in one of several categories: vultures, eagles, hawks and owls. The members of each category have similar adaptations that allow them to survive.

*a*

*b*

(a) Turkey vulture.
(b) Turkey vulture chicks.
(c) Golden eagle.

## VULTURES

The only species of vulture found in the state is the turkey vulture. With weak feet and talons, it is not equipped to kill its own food. Instead it feeds on carrion. Surprisingly, it uses its superb sense of smell as well as its sharp eyes to locate the rotting carcasses.

Carried by rising air currents, the vulture can often be seen circling high in the sky on tilted wings. Upon spotting a carcass, it drops through the air like a huge black stone. Other vultures spotting the dropping form of the bird soon join in for the feast.

*c*

## EAGLES

Measuring up to 7 feet from wingtip to wingtip and weighing as much as 14 pounds, eagles are our largest birds of prey. Although classified with the buteos, their large size gives them title to the term eagle.

The bald eagle is primarily a fish eater. In the fall, more than 600 of these birds may congregate along McDonald Creek in Glacier National Park to feed on spawning kokanee salmon. Not above piracy, our national symbol may harass fish-laden osprey into dropping their catch. After adeptly picking the booty out of mid-air and flying to a favored perch, it proceeds with its meal without even getting wet feet.

While bald eagles are seen primarily in the western mountains, golden eagles may be seen almost anywhere in the state. Golden eagles search for prey from a position high in the sky, almost out of sight. They overtake their victims in a single, long dive that may reach speeds of 150 miles per hour.

More variable in their food habits than the fish eating bald eagle, golden eagles take a variety of insects, small mammals, reptiles and birds. An occasional great-horned owl, magpie or pigeon also may fall victim. However, rabbits, marmots and ground squirrels make up the bulk of their diet.

b            c            d

*a*

*(a) Bald eagle in Glacier National Park.*
*(b) Golden eagle. (c) Red-tailed hawk. (d) Prairie falcon.*

# HAWKS

Montana has 16 species of hawks. The marsh hawk and the osprey both stand alone while the others, depending on their body form and method of hunting, are divided into one of several groups: buteos, accipiters or falcons. Each category of hawk predominates in certain types of habitats and where particular conditions exist.

Buteos are birds of the plains, fields, mountains and open woodlands. Circling high above the plains on broad soaring wings, they search the ground for victims, which usually are rodents. However, oblivious to the dangers of poisonous venom and stinging spray, red-tailed hawks will also kill rattlesnakes and skunks for food.

Unique in a different way, the Swainson's hawk migrates farther than any other North American hawk, flying 11,000 to 17,000 miles from its summer range in northern United States and southern Canada to its winter range in Argentina. While migrating in large flocks, this common summer resident of Montana is believed to eat little or nothing during its journey. Our most numerous wintering hawk is the rough-legged hawk. It is the only buteo with legs feathered to the toes — a characteristic useful to a bird that nests in the Arctic and winters in the cold north.

The sharp-shinned hawk, the Cooper's hawk and the goshawk are three accipiters found in Montana.

They have short, rounded wings and long tail, features that provide them with great maneuverability. Inhabitants of woodlands, they pursue small birds for food.

Hidden by dense foliage, they wait, surveying the underbrush for a slight movement that betrays the presence of a sparrow or warbler. Seeing it, they swoop down, knifing through the branches. In midsong, totally unaware of the presence of the killer, the tiny singer is snatched from its perch by the needle-sharp talons.

Similar to accipiters in their preference for birds, the falcons differ in their habitat requirements and their hunting methods. On long, pointed wings designed for speed, they hunt open country and take their avian prey on the wing. The peregrine falcon, now rare in Montana (see section on Rare and Endangered species), is reputed to be the fastest bird in the world. Like the other falcons, its lightning-fast swoop, timed at more than 200 miles per hour, ends in a brittle explosion of death. During these incredible dives, special contours of its nostrils break the air, enabling it to breathe.

The most common falcon in Montana, the 8½-inch American kestrel is frequently seen hovering over roadside ditches. Unlike its larger relatives, the gyrfalcon, peregrine falcon, prairie falcon and merlin, it feeds primarily on insects.

103

a

b

c

d

(a) American kestrel with mouse
(b) Marsh hawk.
(c) American kestrel.
(d) Prairie falcon on kill.
(e) Common nighthawk.
(f) Gyrfalcon on pheasant kill.
(g) Osprey.
(h) Osprey and nest.

Quartering almost like a bird dog, the marsh hawk glides slowly and silently a few feet above the ground. Suddenly it hesitates, hovers, and drops straight down into the reeds. As likely as not, another mouse has met its end. An ill-timed squeak or rustle may be as costly for a mouse as spending too much time in the open, for the marsh hawk uses its ears as well as its eyes to locate its prey. Endowed with owl-like facial discs, its hearing is excellent.

The marsh hawk is a bird of the grass and brushy marshes. Slim, with long, rounded wings and a long tail, it is capable of incredible aerial maneuvers. Its courtship display is awe-inspiring, consisting of breath-taking dives and loop-the-loops.

On long, narrow soaring wings, the osprey patrols the waterways of western Montana. Upon spotting a fish near the surface, it plunges feet first into the water, impaling the victim on sharp talons and driving it into the water.

Spicules, small spiny growths on the bottoms of its feet, help the osprey grasp its slippery prey. In addition, the outer toe on each foot is reversible and can be rotated to the rear, giving the bird two strongly hooked claws on each side of its prey.

e

f

g

h

# Owls

Often linked with spooks and hobgoblins, owls have been called devils, witches with wings and bad omens. They are often associated with death. "The bird of death," "terror of the night," and "messenger of death" are a few favored phrases authors and poets have used to describe these birds. Because of such literary denunciation owls have been unjustly feared and persecuted throughout the ages.

In recent years, modern wildlife research techniques have enabled biologists to penetrate the mysterious world of these birds and remove the cloak of mystique surrounding them. The results of these studies have revealed owls for what they are—predatory creatures superbly equipped for living on nocturnal rodents.

Like those of the diurnal raptors, the eyes of owls are remarkable organs. Although they are believed to be two or three times as acute as our own, their most astonishing characteristic is their light-gathering ability. A burning candle, 1200 feet distant, provides enough illumination to guide an owl to its target.

In complete darkness, which even their remarkable eyes cannot penetrate, owls can still catch mice — a feat made possible by ears designed for the location of sound. Differing in size and surrounded by facial discs that aid in gathering sound, their ears magnify differences in the strength of the signal to each ear, making it possible to pinpoint the source of the sound.

In contrast to the blinding speed of the diurnal birds of prey, the approach of owls is slow and silent. Fluffy feathers dampen the sound of air passing over and through the feathers. In addition, their wings are large in comparison to their weight, enabling them to fly noiselessly, buoyantly and effortlessly.

Should their remarkable eyes and ears fail to pinpoint their intended victim or should the prey bolt at the last moment because of a slight sound or a passing shadow in the moonlight, owls still have an ace in the hole. Extremely large and strong, their feet and talons allow for some margin of error while attacking.

Montana owls vary in their habitat requirements. While most live in forests or near forest edges, the burrowing owl and the short-eared owl are common in open country. They also differ from the other owls in that they are frequently seen foraging during daylight hours.

Montana owls vary in size. With a wingspan of 60 inches, the great-gray owl of the western mountains is the largest. Running a close second is the great horned owl with its wingspan of 55 inches. Montana's smallest owl is the pygmy owl, which measures a scant 7 inches and weighs 2.5 ounces.

a

b

c

d

*(a) Typical threat posture assumed by many owls. (b) Burrowing owl. (c) Great gray owl. (d) Screech owl. (e) Long-eared owl. (f) Barrel owl.*

e

f

*(a) Young short-eared owl. (b) Great horned owl. (c) Young great horned owls.*

## GREAT HORNED OWLS

Competition among young birds is keen, particularly when speaking of great horned owls. Photographed at the National Bison Range in the month of May, the original clutch size containing the birds at left may have numbered four, but the two shown here managed to oust the others indicating that the availability of food the year this photo was taken may not have been all that abundant. Whether the two larger owlets survive depends on the subsequent provender secured by the parents. Such feed could consist of smaller birds, mice, skunks or other small mammals.

Eggs were laid in wintry mid-March, high in a cottonwood tree in an old hawk nest. Incubation time is about 30 days. Another eight weeks is required to raise them through the early stage of total dependency and on through the highly competitive weeks of adolescence. At the end of this period, the survivors will become one of the most efficient of our avian predators, sometimes known as the winged tiger.

## UPLAND GAME BIRDS

On a brisk autumn morning, a graying hunter shoulders his well-worn, double-barrelled shotgun and follows as his dog bounces through the tall vegetation flanking a gently meandering stream. The shorthair slams to a point and the hunter's pulse quickens. Gun at ready, the veteran nimrod moves into position. But, the expected flush does not occur and the hunter turns to his dog in disappointment.

Suddenly, a cock pheasant explodes from beneath his feet — its coppery body gleaming in the morning sun, its light gray wings clawing for air and its streaming tail undulating with every wingbeat.

Two shots ring out in rapid succession but the bird sails on, unruffled, untouched. Smiling at his opening-day jitters, the hunter reminisces about similar misses in past seasons spanning half a century. Philosophically, he moves on, knowing there will be other birds, other days and other seasons.

Similar scenes take place all across the state of Montana on the opening day of pheasant season as hunters of all ages and walks of life try their hand at bagging Montana's most popular game bird. Its exciting flush, noisy flight, large size, colorful plumage and excellent taste all contribute to its popularity and familiarity. In fact the ring-necked pheasant is so familiar that hunters may forget that the pheasant was imported from Asia around the turn of the century and is not a native of Montana.

Contrary to what today's hunters find, early settlers in Montana discovered an abundance of native game birds. At the time, prairie grasslands were filled with sharp-tailed grouse, and sagebrush slopes teemed with sage grouse. But, as the settlers began to turn the prairie sod and convert huge tracts of native grasslands and sagebrush into crop lands, native grouse populations declined, leaving in the wake of the plow, vast areas that were virtually devoid of game birds.

Unhappy with the changes, avid sportsmen followed the example provided by other states and began importing ring-neck pheasants. The results of the earliest introductions, which occurred prior to 1895, were reported in 1902 in the first biennial statement of the Fish and Game Commission. "These birds," said the report, "have been imported and turned loose year after year, but their propogation has been anything but successful." Nevertheless, the Montana Department of Fish and Game bowed to pressure from sportsmen. Between 1909 and 1929 about 7,000 pheasants were introduced to various habitats across the state.

Releases were made first in Lincoln, Flathead, Lake, Ravalli and Teton counties. Subsequently birds were liberated near Glasgow and Lewistown, and then across the state. By the mid-1920s pheasants were plentiful in some areas of the state and Montana's sportsmen were requesting a season. The first season, granted in 1928, met with limited success as only a few birds were taken.

The population continued to increase to a high in the early 1940s and then declined sharply to a low in 1945. The early buildup is believed to have been the result of ideal weather, abundant cover and plentiful food.

Since the early '40s, land-use practices have changed radically. Larger farms, more intensive farming practices, and the widespread use of herbicides have eliminated much of the tall, dense cover and the weedy "edge" needed by pheasants.

The ring-neck pheasant is not the only foreign game bird in Montana. Hungarian or gray partridge first were released by private individuals or groups prior to 1915. A few years later, between 1922 and 1926, the Montana Fish and Game Commission purchased 6,000 huns and distributed them throughout the state. The birds adapted well to various habitats within the prairie region and since have become popular with hunters.

As with all upland game-bird populations, the number of huns is limited by climate and vegetative cover. They flourish in cool, moderately dry climates where there is a good mixture of cultivated and non-cultivated land — conditions met by most of northern and eastern Montana.

Although huns are excellent sporting birds, they usually are bagged in conjunction with other game birds such as pheasants or sharptails. Coveys flush as a unit. The explosion of numerous wings and speedy flight often leave the hunter with nothing but spent shells.

Still another Old World game bird that inhabits Montana is the chukar. Originally native to southern Europe, Asia Minor, India, Tibet, China and Mongolia, the chukar was introduced into Montana in 1933 near the Yellowstone River below Glendive. Similar events occurred periodically in 16 counties during the following seven years, but the big push to establish the birds did not come until later. Between 1950 and 1958, 5,000 chukars were released into suitable habitat throughout the state. Although most released birds

a

b

e

c

d

(a) Ring-necked pheasants were introduced into Montana in the early 1880s. (b) A recent import, the turkey, was released near Ekalaka in 1954. (c) Montana's harsh winters have not prevented the turkey from expanding its range. (d) Ruffed grouse chick. (e) The motorboat sound of the ruffed grouse during the courtship period is created by the rapid fanning of its wings.

a

b

c

d

*All grouse have unique displays performed during the mating season. (a) Sharp-tailed grouse. (b) Blue grouse displaying. (c) Sage Grouse. (d) Blue grouse in relaxed state.*

simply disappeared, those in the Fromberg-Red Lodge-Bighorn Canyon area south of Billings have flourished and the area supports a huntable population.

Preferred chukar habitat in Montana consists of sagebrush-juniper or sagebrush-bitterbrush interspersed with cheatgrass and bunchgrasses. Within those broad areas, the birds seek brushy slopes and draws for most activities but may feed in grain fields. Although they inhabit areas of low rainfall, chukars are dependent on free water and require it daily. Drought conditions cause them to congregate around waterholes.

The most limiting factor in chukar distribution is snow fall. Heavy snows cover available food and roosting areas and may have serious adverse affects on the population.

The largest of Montana's non-native game birds is the Merriam's turkey. The first introduction consisted of 13 birds, five gobblers and eight hens; and took place on November 13, 1954, near Capital Rock in the Long Pines area near Ekalaka and in the Beaver Creek area near Ashland. The turkeys flourished, eventually providing stock for transplants to other areas within the state. Today, more than 25 flocks of wild turkeys live within the state.

Turkeys prefer open ponderosa pine forest in rugged terrain and have been most successful where the vegetation mix consists of about one-half ponderosa pine with the other half consisting of a mixture of grasses, deciduous trees and brush. Ideally, these areas are interspersed with small openings and drainage-ways.

Areas of riverbottom habitat, like the Flathead River bottoms of Flathead County, also appear to meet their needs. Evidently, all available habitat is not occupied, because turkeys are continuing to extend their range in many areas.

Unlike the ring-necked pheasants, Hungarian partridges, chukars and turkeys, the five species of Montana grouse are all natives. Originally, grouse filled almost all habitats in the state but, with the coming of the plow, they were eliminated from huge tracts of cultivated lands.

Sharp-tailed grouse are birds of the prairie and brushlands. Although their range has been reduced by heavy grazing and cultivation, they still can be found in areas where mixed grasslands have been maintained. Once widely distributed across the grasslands west of the Continental Divide, they now exist in only three limited and widely separated areas in the Black-

foot, Flathead and Kootenai River valleys. These fragmented populations west of the Divide are highly vulnerable to future development, and they may well disappear within the near future. Statewide, the sharptail will have to depend on well-managed grazing lands and other lands not suitable to the plow.

The sage grouse is, as its name suggests, closely associated with sagebrush. So close in fact, that its original distribution corresponded roughly to that of big sage and related species. Since then, more than 50 percent of its habitat has been taken over by agriculture and livestock grazing. The largest North American grouse, sage grouse are highly specialized birds. Unlike the other upland game birds, they have very thin-walled gizzards incapable of grinding up seeds and other hard material. Consequently, they depend on the leafy parts of sagebrush and other herbaceous plants. As the winter snows cover other vegetation, the birds switch to big sage almost exclusively.

Although it has been reduced in number and is no longer the leading game bird in Montana as it was in pioneer times, the sage grouse is still one of the more important and interesting of Montana's game birds.

The grouse of the forests are the blue, ruffed and spruce grouse. The blue grouse inhabits primarily Douglas fir coniferous forest areas and open slash burns. The ruffed grouse prefers brushy areas in mixed or deciduous forests, while the spruce grouse prefers the deep, wet, coniferous forests of subalpine fir, Engelman spruce, jackpine and lodgepole pine stands.

The grouse populations are tied closely to the conditions of their ranges. The elimination of forest fires from much of the public lands inhabited by the grouse has resulted in an increased density of the understory, much to the detriment of the grouse. Conversely, overgrazing has reduced the herbaceous cover necessary for the successful rearing of broods.

Although listed as an upland game bird by virtue of its family ties, the white-tailed ptarmigan has not been hunted in Montana since it was first protected by game laws in 1931. The sporting qualities of these birds are excellent and there is sound biological evidence to support hunting. But, much of their habitat lies within Glacier National Park, which would limit huntable populations even if hunting were allowed in the state.

The white-tailed ptarmigan confines itself to the alpine and subalpine areas of a few of the higher mountain ranges. Because this habitat is largely inaccessible and not useful to man for any purpose other than recreation, ptarmigan populations probably will remain stable.

a

b

c

d

*(a, b, c, d) Ptarmigan are masters in the art of protective camouflage. As the year progresses, their plumage changes to blend with the season's predominant color. (e) Young flightless calliope hummingbird about thumb-length in size.*

e

# WHITE-TAILED PTARMIGAN

The white-tailed ptarmigan stands unchallenged as the bird that inhabits the most rugged terrain in Montana and also endures the most severe climatic conditions. Its alpine world is at once intriguing and formidable.

The ptarmigan has several physical adaptations that make life possible under the severe conditions imposed on it by its habitat. The most obvious and the most familiar of these attributes is the color change it undergoes each year. In summer, the bird is a mottled brown. As fall turns into winter, the ptarmigan begins losing feathers. The replacements are pure white instead of the mottled brown. By the time winter settles in earnest, the bird is pure white, except for the black bill and eyes, a perfect match for its white surroundings. As spring breaks, the process is reversed and the bird is again a mottled brown. The change of color is triggered mainly by the changing day length, so if the snows come early or late, the bird may be out of phase and exceptionally vulnerable to predators for a short time.

Ptarmigan spend their winter days feeding on the leaves and buds of dwarf willow. Winter nights are spent in burrows in the snow. These snow caves insulate the ptarmigan from the rigorous elements and enable it to survive the intense cold. During storms, the birds may spend several days in these caves, waiting for the storm to abate.

Occasionally, these caves become death traps. Following a warm day, there may be enough moisture in the surface snow to form a tough crust when the temperatures drop at night. Ptarmigan trapped under such a crust for more than a day or two will eventually starve or suffocate.

Still another characteristic of the ptarmigan that helps it in winter is its feathered feet. The feathers on its lower legs and toes not only minimize heat loss from the lower legs but also act like snowshoes by providing more surface area for the bird to walk on in the snow.

# HUMMINGBIRDS

The calliope hummingbird is a bird of superlatives. It has the distinction of being the smallest bird on the entire continent. Its powers of flight are unparalleled by any but other hummingbirds. Its consumption of food in relation to its body size is unsurpassed. And, the amount of affection and admiration accorded it is second to none. Its dazzling iridescent colors and sunny disposition certainly justify its scientific name which means little star.

In addition to the calliope, the rufous hummingbird and the black-chinned hummingbird are seen regularly in Montana. The most brightly colored of Montana's birds, the male hummingbirds are easy to distinguish because of the presence of brightly colored iridescent throat patches called gorgets. The gorget of the calliope is a candy-striped scarlet, while that of the rufous is a solid scarlet. That of the black-chinned is a metallic blue-black. The females are similar to their male counterparts but lack the gorgets, making them much more difficult to identify in the field.

A flying hummer often appears to be changing color with every slight shift of its body, an effect caused by thinly laminated structures in the barbules of its feathers. These structures interfere with the light rays striking the feathers, scattering them and presenting observers with brilliant reds, violets and greens. The gorget of the male shows its most brilliant color in only

*(a & b) With perseverance, hummingbirds can be photographed from a blind, but to lure one to a finger (c) as has Monta Anna Gordon of Bigfork requires dedicated patience. (d) Adults feed their young at precise intervals of about 20 minutes.*

one direction — head-on. Even a slight variance of this angle can make the gorget change from red or violet to black.

Hummers have the greatest output of energy per unit of weight of any known animal except insects in flight. To keep up with their demand for calories, hummers may eat 300 or more times per day. If a human expended energy at the same rate per unit of weight as a hummingbird, he would have to consume the equivalent of 370 pounds of boiled potatoes or 140 pounds of bread every day.

In addition to the large number of calories, which they obtain by sipping nectar from flowers, hummers also need protein. This they obtain by eating small insects and spiders.

When evening comes, hummingbirds find a suitable roosting tree and become torpid, a state more like hibernation than sleep. During torpor, their body temperature may drop almost to that of the surrounding air. If captured during this condition, they may chirp weakly and flap their wings, but they are incapable of flight. In fact, if set back on their perch, they are unable to hold themselves up. During torpor their body temperature rises a degree or two per minute and the respiration and heart rate increase. When their body temperature passes 86 degrees, they are once again able to fly.

Hummingbirds may become torpid at night anytime the temperature drops below about 93 degrees, which

is virtually every night here in Montana. If the air temperature drops to 60 degrees, the torpid bird may save almost 98 percent of the energy it would need to maintain its body temperature at its daytime level.

Even more outstanding than the hummers' fiery colors are their powers of flight. Hummers do it all! They can fly forward, backward, sideways, straight up and straight down as well as any combination of the above. They can pivot, hover and even do backward somersaults. The only thing they cannot do is soar on motionless wings, a feat reserved for larger birds with broader wings.

In most birds, the downstroke of the wing produces the power while the upstroke merely moves the wing into position for another power stroke. In the hummers, both strokes are power strokes, greatly increasing their efficiency and maneuverability.

While hovering, a hummer moves its wings forward and backward in a figure-eight motion rather than an up and down motion. The wing is pivoted 180 degrees between strokes, so the front edge of the wing always cuts the air and provides lift. On the backstroke, the bottom side of the wing is uppermost.

Hummingbirds wings appear to be a blur to observers and with good reason. While hovering, their wings beat about 40 times each second. During certain maneuvers in their courtship flights, their wings may beat up to 200 times per second!

While their powers of flight are great, their ability to walk seems to be nonexistent. When an incubating female wishes to turn her eggs, she flies backward from the eggs to the rim of the nest, turns the eggs, and flies back to her eggs — a distance of less than an inch.

Incubating or brooding females do not become torpid, because the drop in temperature would greatly retard the development of the embryos or young. Similarly, older nestlings do not appear to become torpid when left exposed to the cold night air.

As you can see, hummingbirds are truly remarkable creatures. No wonder they are loved and admired throughout their range.

## HUMMINGBIRD FEEDING YOUNG

From their winter homes in Mexico, hummingbirds return to Montana sometime around the middle of May. Males arrive first. The appearance of the females triggers spectacular courting flights by the males, after which, if successful, the females go off by themselves to build the nest, lay and incubate the eggs and raise the young.

The nest is a neat cuplike structure built of moss, lichens and tiny parts of plants which are held together by cobwebs. It is usually about an inch deep and an inch and a half in diameter.

The two white, bean-sized eggs are laid two days apart and hatch about 20 days later but at different times. If food is scarce, the younger and weaker sibling may starve or be pushed from the nest by the other. The young are fed by regurgitation. The almost fearsome sight of the mother thrusting her long, needle-sharp bill down the throat of her young is reminiscent of a sword-swallowing act.

Young fledge in about three weeks. The female continues to feed them for a couple weeks after they leave the nest. During this time, they must learn to feed themselves. At first, they may probe bark, pale red leaves, signal lights, red labels or anything else that remotely resembles the color, size and shape of a flower.

*a*

*Brightly colored feeders attract hummingbirds.*

# HUMMINGBIRD AT FEEDER

Hummers readily adapt to humans and can be attracted by plantings of suitable flowers and by feeders offering sugar water. They seem to prefer scarlet tubular flowers, although they also use orange, purple, yellow and white flowers. Favored flowers include the fuchsias, honeysuckle, morning glories, delphiniums, columbines, phlox and petunias. Sugar water feeders should be located in a conspicuous place and filled with a solution of four parts water to one part sugar. They should be cleaned periodically to prevent the growth of harmful fungi.

*b*

*c*

*d*

# WOODPECKERS

The birds in this group are easily recognizable as woodpeckers. And, pecking wood is indeed what they are designed to do. With stout, chisel-shaped beaks fastened to heavy skulls and driven with strong neck muscles, they are capable of drilling into solid wood. Short, stout legs and strong toes tipped with sharp, curved claws enable them to cling tenaciously to vertical tree trunks. This position is further secured by propping their stiff central tail feathers against the rough bark.

A familiar sound in the timbered woods of Montana, the staccato drumming of a drilling woodpecker may mean more than a bird with a healthy appetite. The sound also is used by the birds in marking their territories and in courting females.

Of the 11 species of woodpeckers seen in Montana, ranging in size from the 15-inch pileated woodpecker to the 5¾-inch downy woodpecker, 10 are known to breed here. Only the nest of the white-headed woodpecker remains to be discovered.

**Although not as plentiful in winter as in summer, the insects they feed on can be found under bark and in rotting wood. Consequently most woodpeckers remain in Montana year round. Always ready for a handout they are easily attracted to suet stations.**

While seeking out insects and insect larvae in the crevices of bark and rotting wood, woodpeckers often start at the base of a tree and work their way up. They may go straight up or spiral around the trunk. Upon reaching the top, they drop to the base of the next tree and begin again.

*(b, c, d) Woodpeckers, like other "cavity-nesting" birds, rely extensively on old snags to rear their young. Examples are (left to right), the red-shafted flicker, yellow-bellied sapsucker, and hairy woodpecker.*

In contrast to the other woodpeckers, flickers frequently feed on the ground, searching for insects, insect larvae and their favorite food, ants. Champion ant-eaters, they consume more ants than any other North American bird.

The presence of a series of horizontal rows of holes in the bark of an aspen, birch, or other tree, indicates the presence of either the Williamson's or the yellow-bellied sapsucker. They feed both on the sap that flows from the wounds and on the insects that are trapped by the sticky ooze. Other birds, like the hummingbird, also may frequent the banquet provided by the sapsuckers. While the damage to the tree looks severe, negative effects are mostly cosmetic and the wounds soon heal over.

Because they are the only birds in Montana capable of drilling in solid wood, the woodpeckers are important to the survival of other cavity-nesting birds. While chickadees and a few other species are capable of excavating rotting wood, wrens, bluebirds, swallows, American kestrel, starling and screech owls must locate existing holes. By drilling a new nesting cavity every year and abandoning the old residence, woodpeckers provide these other birds with a variety of nesting cavities.

*Western tanager.*

# SONGBIRDS

Even before the first hint of dawn reveals the coming of another spring day, the first tentative song filters through the trees. The soloist is soon joined by another. The duet grows to a trio, then a quartet and soon a swell of music permeates the forest, emanating from a multitude of unseen singers.

Music lovers can find similar choirs in virtually all habitats of Montana. In fact, it would be difficult, if not impossible to locate an area in the state without its bird ensemble. In most areas, listeners are rewarded by simultaneous serenades from a hundred or more little songsters.

Of all the birds in the state, 45 percent belong to a group called the passerines or perching birds. Because of their beautiful songs and amazing repertoires, the members of this group are commonly called songbirds. With more than 900 different songs recorded within the species, the appropriately named song sparrow is the champion musician. There are, however, songbirds that are totally incapable of emitting anything even resembling a song.

Although we commonly associate singing with gaiety, birds do not sing because they are happy. Rather, they sing to communicate. Songs establish territories, attract and court mates; they identify individuals, keep flocks together and warn of danger. Although birds sing primarily in the spring, many sing throughout the year.

When used in the defense of a territory, songs are powerful tools. Researchers have taken caged birds into the woods and let them sing. The caged birds were able to keep other birds away from their "territories" just by their songs. In some cases, the caged birds even succeeded in driving out a bird that had already established a territory in the area, something a wild, free bird rarely is able to do.

Songbirds inhabit all vegetative types in the state, but the various woodlands contain the greatest number of individuals. Here may be found the greatest number of species, the best songsters and the most brightly colored individuals. The reasons are simple. Being a three dimensional habitat instead of a two dimensional one like the prairie, the woodlands have more niches and can support a greater number and variety of plants and insects.

In the woodlands where visibility is limited by thick vegetation, birds communicate almost exclusively by songs. Here, the only means of recognizing unseen neighbors is the slight variations in their songs. Potential mates are located and won over by rich melodious singing.

Not limited by obstructing shrubbery, birds of the prairie communicate by visual means as well as with songs. Horned larks and longspurs sing their tinkling songs while flying high above their territories. Meadowlarks pick prominent perches and thrust out their bright yellow chests while vocalizing. The voices of grassland birds are higher than those of their woodland counterparts and carry well in the open.

The absence of trees and tall shrubs makes prairie birds highly vulnerable to avian predators. Consequently, they usually have mottled brown backs to help them blend into the ground. Their habit of freezing at the first sign of danger heightens the effectiveness of their protective coloration.

Nests are built on the ground or in low bushes. In either case, the birds often take circuitous routes back to their nests or drop to the ground some distance from the nest. Then they run along the ground the last several feet to avoid revealing the nest site.

Birds of the prairie also face more extreme environmental conditions than do the birds of the woodlands. Here there is no tall vegetation to protect them from gale winds and torrential rains. Snow and ice, fire and drought take their toll.

Regardless of where they are found, songbirds are master nest builders. The dome-shaped nest of the meadowlark blends in with the prairie grasses just as well as the intricately woven nest of the yellow warbler fits into its woodland world. Most nests contain some grasses, usually woven together in a basket-shaped bowl. Many species use amounts of mud to "cement" their nests together, but many also use cobwebs to hold the structure intact. Nests usually are lined with soft materials — mosses, fine grasses and down.

In contrast to natural environments found in the woodlands and prairies, the artificial environments of suburbia also attract birds. The mixture of lawns, gardens, flower beds, trees, concrete, asphalt and buildings has appealed to several species.

Perhaps the best known of these suburban birds is the ubiquitous robin. Robins build their nests astride forks in horizontal branches or in crotches near trunks of trees of saplings, but just as readily will occupy nooks and crannies on porches, barns, sheds, outhouses and bridges.

The story is told of a robin that built its nest in the south end of a shed that covered a table in a railroad terminal upon which locomotives frequently were turned. When her end of the shed was turned to the north, she built another nest in the temporary south end. As the ends changed from day to day, she soon had two nests and two sets of eggs. The last reports had her sitting on whichever nest happened to be the south end of the shed at the time.

Another familiar species is the barn swallow. Instead of hollow trees used by its ancestors, the barn swallow now uses man-made structures almost exclusively to protect its mud nests from predators and the elements.

In addition to the abundant nooks and crannies inadvertently created by human activities, bird lovers in suburbia provide bird houses in the hope of attracting feathered friends. Wrens, tree swallows, starlings and house sparrows have all responded to this enticement and are totally at home in this environment.

Similarly, by planting ornamental shrubs and bushes, men have increased the food supply of some birds. One bird whose habits have been modified considerably by such activities is the Bohemian waxwing. Nomads in winter, these birds wander erratically in search of berries, which are their main source of food. Because men have planted shrubs and trees that produce persistent berries, like the mountain ash, crab apple and dogwood, waxwings no longer are forced by inadequate food supplies to move further south. As a result, tight formations of these birds are seen frequently in Montana during winter, wheeling and diving like fighter planes on maneuvers.

(a) Steller's jay.
(b) Black-billed magpie.
(c) Mountain bluebird.
(d) Savannah sparrow.
(e) Evening grosbeak.

(f) Mountain chickadee.
(g) Tree swallow.
(h) House sparrow.
(i) Tree swallow.
(j) American robin.

(k) Bohemian waxwing.
(l) Clark's nutcracker.
(m) Red-shafted flicker.
(n) Yellow-rumped or
Audubon warbler.

(o) Loggerhead shrike.
(p) Cassin's finch.
(q) Eastern kingbird.

a

b

c

d

## WESTERN MEADOWLARK

Most often seen perched on a fencepost, its yellow breast shining in the sun, its head thrown back and a bubbling song emerging from its vocal cords, the meadowlark is Montana's state bird. It is so abundant and well-liked throughout the West that it is also honored as the state bird in Kansas, Wyoming, Nebraska, North Dakota and Oregon.

As the spring snow is leaving the ground, male meadowlarks begin to establish nesting territories. Each male sings from a prominent perch along the boundaries of his territory to warn other males that this territory is occupied. The song also serves to welcome any female to his terrain.

The dome-shaped nest is built on the ground and has a side entrance. Like many of the ground nesters attempting to deceive predators, the meadowlark often lands 20 or 30 feet away from the nest and walks home. Their three to seven eggs are heavily spotted. The young are fed mostly insects and remain in the nest for about 10 days. Even after fledging, the parents continue to feed the young for about another two weeks.

Meadowlarks are more at home on the ground than in the air. When flushed, they alternate rapid wingbeats with short glides and soon drop back to the ground. While walking on the ground, they often flick their tails open and shut. Their mottled brown backs serve to camouflage them from avian predators while searching for weed seeds or insects to eat.

Although most meadowlarks move south with the approach of winter, a few hardy, or foolhardy, souls usually can be seen along the roadsides even in the dead of winter.

## GRAY JAY

The gray jay, alias Canada jay, camp robber and whisky jack, is common in the cool coniferous forests of the western part of the state. It sometimes frequents campgrounds and logging camps in the hope of pilfering scraps of food. It stores these scraps of frozen meat, suet or hide by glueing them into balls with its saliva and hiding them among needles.

It nests early, in March or April, building its twiggy, feather-lined nest in a conifer and laying its three to five greenish, gray-spotted eggs. The gray jay frequently incubates its eggs with snow on its back.

(a) Western meadowlark.
(b) Gray jay.
(c) American dipper.
(d) Young dippers in nest.
(e & f) Barn swallow.

e

f

# AMERICAN DIPPER

This chunky, slate-covered, robin-sized bird with its stubby tail is well adapted to the icy-cold streams of western Montana. Covered with soft, thick plumage and endowed with special oil glands, the dipper can negotiate icy waters with impunity. In fact, it can even be seen diving under the ice in search of aquatic insects.

The dipper is completely oriented to life along Montana's mountain streams where it can be recognized easily by its distinctive habit of bobbing up and down while standing on a handy rock along the shoreline or in midstream. Like the harlequin duck, it uses its ability to walk along the bottom of the stream while probing for food. When foraging up or downstream, it flies over the water, rarely taking any shortcuts over land.

Its nest is a bulky ball of moss with a side entrance and is usually located on a rock wall, under a bridge, behind a waterfall or in some other location near the water. Perpetually damp, the moss may remain alive and form a living, growing nest.

# BARN SWALLOW

The barn swallow is a familiar bird throughout the state, loved and admired by most. In the past, the destruction of its nest was believed to bring fire, lightning or even death to the house or its inhabitants.

Its mud nests are a familiar sight in buildings, under bridges, and in and around other man-made structures. Both the male and female participate in nest building. They visit nearby seeps to obtain small pellets of mud which they carry back to the nest site in their bills. The lower layers of the nest usually have quantities of grass mixed in with the pellets of mud. The mixture of mud, grass and saliva sticks extremely well, enabling the swallows to build their nest on almost any vertical surface.

The completed nest is lined with feathers and the female lays from four to six white eggs with reddish spots. When the young hatch, the adults feed them with insects.

Like the rest of the swallow family, barn swallows have extremely long wings and are excellent fliers. Their short legs and weak feet are used only for perching. Their bills are short, flat and triangular, but their mouths are large, enabling them to scoop flying insects directly out of the air.

a

b

(a) Yellow-headed blackbird.

(b) Black-billed magpie.

# YELLOW-HEADED BLACKBIRD

Appropriately named, the yellow-headed blackbird nests in dense colonies, occasionally having as many as 25 nests in 15 square feet. Each nest is constructed of water-soaked vegetation which shrinks and clings tenaciously to the reeds. The nests look like open bowls and are hung from the reeds, usually over the water. From three to five whitish, speckled eggs are laid and incubated by the female. The young are fed mostly insects.

Some members of the blackbird family, which also includes the orioles, have beautiful songs — not so the yellow-headed blackbird. Described by some ornithologists as a series of low rasping notes ending in a long descending buzz, its song is hardly musical. Less kindly listeners have compared it to the sound made by a very rusty gate.

# BLACK-BILLED MAGPIE

Several large black and white birds with long tails scatter as you round a turn in the road. A quick glance as you pass confirms your suspicions — an unlucky jackrabbit is the reason for the gathering. A glance in the rear view mirror shows the black-billed magpies already returning to their banquet.

Part of nature's solid-waste-disposal crew, magpies speed the recycling process of dead animals as well as performing the cosmetic function of cleaning our highways. Besides carrion, these omnivorous birds eat small birds (as well as eggs and young), crawfish, small mammals, insects (crickets, grasshoppers, grubs and larvae), fruits, berries and green leaves.

Magpies are found in or near open country with patches of heavy brush and occasional trees in which they throw together the haphazard mass of sticks we call a nest. Six to nine greenish eggs are laid in the dome-shaped structures. During early spring, a peek in the side entrance will show wall to wall magpies as the young approach fledging. After the young have fledged, the adults find another suitable spot for a nest and build a new one, leaving the old one for screech owls, kestrels or anything else that cares to take up residence.

In spite of the persecution by man, this rather raucous member of the jay family is in no danger of extinction. In fact, this extremely adaptable bird seems to prefer civilization — perhaps it just likes the audience.

115

a

# REPTILES AND AMPHIBIANS

b

*(a) Rattlesnake prepared to strike.*

*(b) Rattle does not always proceed a strike.*

The most significant factor controlling the lives of reptiles and amphibians is temperature. Lacking the internal mechanisms that help birds and mammals maintain a constant body temperature regardless of environmental temperatures, the body temperatures of these animals fluctuate to some degree with that of their surroundings. Only by seeking out areas with temperatures within their comfort zone can they regulate their body temperatures.

Because of this inability to regulate internal temperature, amphibians and reptiles emerge from the water or leave the shelter of a fallen log or rock crevice to feed only when temperatures are within their comfort zone. On the cool days of spring and fall, they may be active only during the heat of the day. In summer, blazing heat may curtail their activities to the cooler evenings.

To survive harsh Montana winters, these creatures must find an environment that does not freeze. Most amphibians accomplish this by burrowing in the mud along the shore or at the bottom of a body of water. Some of the salamanders and the more land-loving toads may pass the winter snug in a rotting log. Because they normally inhabit water, it is not surprising that turtles also pass the winter encased in the bottom ooze of lakes or ponds. But, terrestrial lizards and snakes wait out the freezing temperatures in underground sanctuaries, well below frost-line.

Limited primarily by this inability to cope well with cold weather, the number and variety of reptiles and amphibians in Montana is small. In contrast to the state's 378 species of birds and 107 species of mammals, there are only 33 different species of reptiles and amphibians in Montana. Of the seventeen species of reptiles, three are turtles, four are lizards and ten are snakes. Five salamanders and eleven species of frogs and toads make up the sixteen types of amphibians.

Another difference between the birds and mammals and the reptiles and amphibians is the degree of parental care given the young. Mammalian mothers will guard offspring with their lives until the young can fend for themselves. Many avian parents build carefully constructed nests or seek out protected caves in which to lay and incubate their eggs. The hatchlings depend on the adults for food and protection for varying periods of time.

In contrast, the amphibians lay their eggs in large masses in the water and then leave the eggs to hatch by themselves and the young to make their own way. Similarly, female reptiles bury their eggs and then abandon them. Hatchlings must dig their way out and brave the elements and numerous predators alone. Even among the snakes that give birth to live young, abandonment occurs immediately after birth. Young are left to their own devices.

## WESTERN RATTLESNAKE

His name is Rattler.

Rocky outcroppings, stream courses, ledges and talus slopes are his favorite haunts. Being cold-blooded, he is active only when the temperature is right. Hot weather as well as cold will drive him underground so his mid-summer hunting takes place in the morning or evening when it is neither too hot nor too cold. He often can be seen sunning on a rock or absorbing the radiant energy from a road in the cooler weather.

His hunting style is the waiting game and Rattler plays it well. Heat sensitive "pits" located between his eyes and his nostrils, help him locate his warm-blooded prey. A lightning fast strike and a shot of venom terminate the hunt. The small mammal, bird, or lizard is swallowed whole.

A rattlesnake is born live with a blunt horny button at the tip of its tail. Each time it sheds its skin, a new segment is added to its rattle. While it is young, it may shed its skin three or four times a year — depending on how much food it eats and how fast it grows.

Rattlesnakes come in many shades and sizes — all of them dangerous. But, contrary to popular opinion, they do not lie in wait behind logs and rocks to ambush unsuspecting humans. Although they are almost always willing to retreat if given a chance, they will strike when badgered or when a hand or foot is thrust at them without warning. When encountering them in the wild, watch from a safe distance and allow them to retreat. Rattlesnakes also have their place in the world.

# Hog-nosed Snake

The hog-nosed snake is a bluffer. Although it makes a great show of puffing itself up, hissing, coiling and acting dangerous, it is harmless and rarely bites. If the bluff fails, it may roll over on its back and play dead — mouth open and tongue extended. The turned up snout is diagnostic and aids the snake in burrowing into the gravelly or sandy soil it prefers.

# Racer

The racer can be found throughout the state primarily along stream courses that pass through open country and breaks in timbered areas. Fast for a snake, it can travel up to three or four miles per hour. Unlike most snakes, the racer crawls with its head elevated and is diurnal rather than nocturnal. Its food consists mainly of rodents, frogs, young birds, insects and other snakes.

# Painted Turtle

Photographed while sunning itself on a log at the National Bison Range near Moise, this painted turtle clearly exhibits the brilliant red and yellow markings that identify it. The most widespread and common of Montana's turtles, it inhabits ponds and marshes across the state. Montana's other two turtles, the snapping turtle and the spiny softshell, are found in a few of the southeastern counties.

# Pacific Tree Frog

Hatched from eggs laid in gelatinous masses and deposited in water, Pacific tree frogs begin life as gill-breathing, tailed creatures. As they grow and develop, the tadpoles gradually lose their tails and develop legs. Their gills also atrophy and lungs develop. When fully mature, the frogs can live either on land or in the water, absorbing oxygen through lungs while on land and through thin, smooth skin while in the water.

Chiefly a ground dweller, the Pacific tree frog is usually found among low vegetation near water in the mountains and coniferous forests of western Montana. Although their skin is rich in glands which serve to keep it moist, prolonged exposure to sun or other dessicating influences will result in death.

Listen for choruses of these frogs near marshes, lakes, ponds, roadside ditches, reservoirs, slow woodland streams, meadows and grasslands during the spring breeding period.

*a*

*b*

*c*

*d*

*e*

*f*

*(a) Hog-nosed snake.*
*(b) Garter snake.*
*(c) Racer.*
*(d & e) Painted turtle.*
*(f) Pacific tree frog.*

# FISH AND FISHERIES

a

b

c

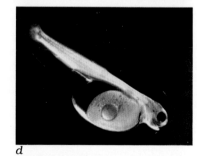

d

Inside the tiny egg, a life had been growing for the last five months, developing, as it grew, a miniscule mouth containing glands now capable of secreting an enzyme. This solvent-like fluid began dissolving the confining membrane of the egg. Simultaneously, the embryo had begun a vigorous movement, swishing its head back and forth, creating a weak spot on the surface of the egg. The time was ripe now for it to break free of the encompassing membrane and enter the world.

But something had gone wrong, and this particular fish emerged head first. The elastic membrane that once had served to protect life now vanquished life. The fish died of suffocation: air was restricted from passing into the body just above the gills.

Fortunately this abnormal emergence depicted by the accompanying picture represents a rarity — a one-in-a-thousand chance. For most fish there is a very high possibility of survival from conception until they reach the fingerling stage. At least that's true at fish hatcheries such as the one located at Somers, Montana.

The idea of fish hatcheries in Montana has been around for a long time thanks largely to a remnant of a continental ice sheet, which occupied Montana as recently as 12,000 years ago. The ice sheet created a barrier to fish in many high-country lakes and streams; scientists believed they could augment the relatively sparse fisheries through the construction of a series of hatcheries.

Montana's first hatchery was built in Bozeman in 1896 followed by the construction of one in Anaconda in 1906 and the Somers fish hatchery in 1912.

At the time the goal was to plant as many fish in as many different waters as was feasible. Today, the thrust has changed as knowledge of fish ecology has improved. Studies have shown that the key to better fishing is to allow natural regulation to govern fish populations and protect the habitat in which they live. In fact research conducted on the Madison River during the early 1970s indicated that planting programs to supplement native populations actually cut wild populations by about one-half. Depletion was the result of overcrowding and stress. As a result, fish no longer are planted to augment existing native populations that are healthy. Rather, fish are planted in areas where natural populations never existed because of barriers such as the relatively recent (geologically speaking) ice age, and in areas that have an abundance of suitable habitat. They also are planted in areas where natural spawning areas have been destroyed by man such as in areas surrounding Libby Dam. Construction of this northwestern Montana dam destroyed habitat for many species of wildlife.

One biologist said the purpose of today's stocking program "is to produce smaller fish for stocking lakes and reservoirs that have adequate conditions for fish growth but inadequate conditions for natural reproduction." Even with this philosophy Montana's seven state-operated hatcheries still plant more than seven million fish annually.

The task of providing fish for such areas is no simple one, and the specific procedures require dedication and an immense amount of work. As conducted at hatcheries such as the one at Somers, work begins each fall when fish managers collect live salmon and

(a) Salmon eggs raised in Montana hatchery.
(b) Death results when salmon emerge head first.
(c) Tail first is normal orientation.
(d) Salmon fry with yolk sac.

manually extract and combine eggs with the milt. Because eggs and milt are viable for only a few minutes, these steps must be conducted on site. Collecting areas include such spawning sites as Lake Mary Ronan, Swan Lake and the Bigfork Power House. Licensed fishermen are then eligible to receive these fish because salmon die shortly after spawning.

After collection, fertilized eggs are taken back to the hatchery where they are measured. This procedure must be conducted within the first 24 hours and is performed because the size of the eggs varies from location to location. By measuring a few eggs and then placing them in a container of known volume, the total number of eggs, which may number in the thousands, can be estimated.

The period following the initial fertilization is a critical time and must be monitored closely. For four to five weeks they cannot be bumped or disturbed in any way. Water trickles through special baskets and simulates the conditions nature provides in her redds. Redds are natural spawning areas of soft gravel beds touched by trickling water.

Within four to five weeks, depending on the temperature of the water, eyes start to develop and can be seen when closely examined. This period of development is referred to as the eye stage, and is illustrated by one of the accompanying photographs.

Eggs that are not fertilized will not exhibit this eye and it is imperative they be removed. This procedure is a manual one and is performed by using a rubber suction bulb. Dead eggs attract slime which could kill eyed eggs.

After separation, the further growth of eggs at this stage often is inhibited by placing them in cold water. Managers want to coordinate the time "fry" or young fish emerge from their eggs with the break-up of ice on surrounding lakes.

Prior to planting, the yolk sac (illustrated in photos) must be absorbed. Once the food contained here is exhausted, these half-inch long fish begin to exhibit a tendency to surface, where they seek plankton. If planted at this stage they could forage for themselves. Still, managers sometimes prefer to hold them until they reach the fingerling stage.

Plantings in 16 different lakes of more than one million fry by the Somers Hatchery generally take place between late April and early June. With such a large planting it is obvious that few fish emerge head first. Most emerge tail first where they live to see a new home in the wild. Here, a vast majority become food for mink, fish and birds, and a rare few grow to become the salmon in anglers' creels.

*a*

*b*

*c*

*d*

*(a) The joys of a Montana stream in summer.*

*(b) Brook trout.*

*(c) Rainbow trout.*

*(d) Grayling spawning.*

119

# SEASONS: CHANGE FOR SURVIVAL

a

*The McDonald Creek eagle congregation (near Glacier Park) has been created by artificial conditions, but most view it as an acceptable by-product of environmental manipulation. It has replaced hundreds of other congregations eliminated by man's interference.*

b

c

# MCDONALD EAGLE CONGREGATION

by Bert Gildart

Daylight was just beginning to creep down the cold valley floor when the first bald eagle flapped its broad wings and dove down hard. A quick thrust into the water with its sharp claws and out came a salmon wriggling in its talons. The eagle returned to its perch to feed.

Soon another eagle followed the first, then another and yet another. By the time the sun crept over the surrounding mountain peaks, I could see 38 of these large white-headed birds. Some were soaring overhead, some were wading in the stream, while still others perched majestically on stout limbs eating their recent catches.

But that wasn't all the eagles. Just around the river bend were more. In fact, one Glacier Park naturalist counted more than 600 of these majestic birds in a single day. And that's a lot of eagles when you realize most people don't see an eagle during the entire year. Some don't even see an eagle in their lifetime.

Eagles once lived in many parts of the United States, and large concentrations were common. But a growing nation of farmers and ranchers shot, poisoned, and trapped them. At that time little was understood about the importance of predators in controlling the populations of rabbits and ground squirrels. And so eagles were killed until only about 600 nest sites remained south of the Canadian border. Not until a few years ago was it declared illegal to destroy them. Another problem was that as cities grew larger and larger, rivers became polluted, and eagles were unable to find food at those places.

Interestingly, at exactly the same time people were making it so hard for eagles, they were also creating a situation that would help bald eagles many years later, the reasons for which we will explain in a moment. No one realized this would happen, but the pleasant result is that during October and November, more bald eagles come to Glacier National Park than to any place in the United States except Alaska.

All this has happened in the last 50 years for, historically, only a few nesting pairs of eagles ever came to Glacier. For most, this has become a very happy situation. Visitors like to know that here, for at least a short time, eagles are safe from the unwarranted pursuits of a few individuals. So they come from all over the country to watch the majestic bird that was made the symbol of our country so many years ago.

If visitors stay long enough, they may watch as an immature eagle grabs a salmon from one of the older eagles. Or, they may see a young eagle as it wades into the river and hooks a fish with its beak. Young eagles aren't good at swooping down and snatching fish from the water, and this is the way they must get their food.

Another day eagles may be seen chasing one another from their perches. For eagle watchers, each day brings something new.

But why are the eagles here? To understand this question we must go back a few years.

In 1916, biologists were starting to realize that much wildlife was being destroyed. To help restore fish, a part of the vanishing wildlife, conservationists became interested in fish planting.

The kokanee salmon, though it had never occured in Flathead Lake, was known by anglers to be delicious, and it was planted in 1916. But the fish didn't stay in the lake year-round and it is the salmon's travels that would eventually attract eagles.

When kokanee salmon are four years old, they have neared the end of their life. There is just one more thing they can do. Inside them hormones initiate a series of reactions that tell them it is time to spawn. Each fall salmon that have reached maturity begin the month-long swim to Glacier Park where they find a few streams that have soft gravel beds. With tails and bodies, they move small rocks forming beds that will protect the developing eggs.

Already tired from their upstream struggle, salmon grow weaker and weaker after spawning. Beating their bodies against rocks rubs away the slippery coating on their scales that protects them against infection, and in about two weeks these salmon have aged rapidly and will die.

Eagles know that at this time salmon are easy to catch, and it didn't take them long to discover this spot in Glacier. By 1939 the word was out among the eagles. The number of eagles grew until hundreds arrive each fall.

**Other animals come to help clean the waters and banks of dead fish. Grizzly bears, coyotes, many species of waterfowl and a variety of different species of gulls show up at the salmon feed. Occasionally it even attracts deer!** One fall, Glacier biologist David Shea noted two deer had joined the eagles along the shore of the river.

With so much food to catch, it's easy to understand why eagles and other species of wildlife congregate each fall in Glacier. But what would happen if the river were to suddenly become polluted? Obviously the salmon would no longer spawn in Glacier and the eagles

and all the other animals would stop coming to this river. For eagle watchers it's not a pleasant thought. But that's exactly what may happen.

Just north of Glacier, connecting with the same stream through which the salmon must travel, a mining company wants to develop a mine site where whole mountain sides will be stripped away for coal. Conservationists believe silt drifting down from this area will pollute the Flathead River system. If that were to happen it is believed that in a few more years there would be no new groups of spawning salmon. Learning this, I made a number of trips to Glacier in one season to make sure I had witnessed the show at its best.

My last trip to the park was in mid-December but searching the familiar perches and scanning the skies overhead, I didn't see a single eagle. Here, only a few short weeks ago, I had stood as dozens of eagles swooped down to pluck salmon.

Up and down the river there had been hundreds of eagles, and I was amazed to see that every last one them had gone. Why I was surprised I don't know, for as I stared down into the water now rimmed with ice I could see that the salmon too were gone. In a few short months, they had traveled 60 miles upstream, spawned, died, and served as a valuable food source for other animals.

It was a simple lesson. When the salmon are gone, the eagles must move on.

# RITES OF SPRING

As the pulse of spring quickens, their dances warm the cold earth and their calls reverberate among the blustery winds. These are the grouse and their courtly, measured posturing stirs the imagination of all who see it. It inspired the plains Indian, who, knowing fine choreography when he saw it, adapted it to his own rituals of welcoming spring and initiating courtship.

Courtship ceremonies of the grouse occur throughout Montana. The sharp-tailed grouse and the sage grouse are the dancers of the wide horizons displaying on the wild dancefloors of the Big Sky. Performers of the forests are the ruffed grouse and the blue grouse. From theaters hidden in the foliage, they call and strut to the whisper of the wind in the leaves and the backdrop of songbird musicians.

While the forest grouse conduct solitary courtships, with the males calling and displaying in isolation, the grouse of the prairies and plains perform in concert. Ardent males gather on traditional communal dancing grounds in the false dawn to coax demure hens with their booming and hooting. It is

a

b

c

*Age-old wildlife rites may still be seen and heard across Montana. Sharp-tail (a and b) and sage grouse (c) in their annual spring performances.*

not simply because they are more social than their forest kin, nor is it because good dancing grounds are so scarce that they must be shared. Rather, it is because a lone suitor would be but a small speck in the sea of grass and the sweep of sky, his posturing unnoticed and his call drifting aimlessly on the wind.

121

a

# MIGRATION

For centuries, men have watched the seasonal appearance and disappearance of birds and wondered where they came from and where they went. Ancient Greek observers suggested birds lived on the moon for several months of the year. Another popular and equally outlandish belief was that birds hibernated in the mud along lakes and streams, just as do frogs.

Today we have a sharper focus on this mystery though many questions remain, and the processes involved in migration are still theoretical. The most obvious question is, what triggers migration? Scientists believe one step involves fat storage to supply the bird with the necessary energy for the flight. Changing day length, or photoperiod, stimulates the production of hormones that in turn causes the buildup of fat. Some birds, such as the warblers and the hummingbirds, may double their weight while accumulating fat. Once the bird is physiologically ready for migration, cold weather triggers the departure for warmer climes.

While these stimuli are known to initiate migration, they do not answer nearly all the questions or explain all situations. Unexplained is the bird's urge to migrate north in the spring when the weather is warming. Also unexplained is why a bird living in the tropics where the day length is nearly constant, should suddenly desire a move north. Moreover it does not explain why shorebirds migrate in August, long before cold weather sets in.

Another obvious but still unanswered question is one of direction. How do birds find their way?

b

*(a) They bring the sky to life.*

*(b) Swans passing over Freeze Out Lake.*

Apparently, different birds use different methods of orientation and navigation. Waterfowl apparently use the sun and stars to direct themselves. This we conclude from noting that they are thrown off course by cloudy weather. Other birds seem to use landmarks — migration routes frequently follow coastlines, rivers or mountain ranges.

Still another method of navigation that influences the route chosen by birds is the earth's magnetic field. Although proposed as a method of orientation for more than a century, not until 1969 did anyone pro-

vide evidence that supported the theory. Although we are capable of finding the trajectory of a spaceship launched to the moon, the last chapter concerning bird navigation has yet to be written.

Most of Montana's smaller birds feed and rest by day and migrate by night. Larger birds that are secretive by day, such as the rails and the snipe, also migrate by night. Many birds, such as loons, grebes, waterfowl, shorebirds, hawks, eagles and pelicans may fly either by day or night. Those that migrate mainly by day include small birds of strong flight, such as swifts, swallows and hummingbirds, which can feed while on the wing. Crows, jays, waxwings, shrikes and blackbirds, horned larks and pine grosbeaks are also day migrants.

The distance traveled each day varies considerably. The robin is a slow but steady migrant, following the 38° isotherm north in the spring at an average of about 36 miles per day. The average distance covered per day by small songbirds is 80 to 100 miles. Waterbirds and shorebirds travel much further — an average of 480 to 1000 miles per flight. Most migrants do not fly night after night. Many may rest and feed for several days in an area before resuming their flight.

Weather plays an important part in the speed of migration. Strong head winds will greatly retard the progress of migrants and will ground smaller species. In contrast, a good tail wind will accelerate the process. Many birds seem to select these nights and altitudes of flight that offer favorable winds. Waterfowl and shorebirds seem to select winds of greater velocity than those selected by smaller birds.

**Where do the summer residents of Montana go in the winter? Once again that depends on the species to some extent, and on the individual bird. Some winter in southern California and some in Texas. But, the vast majority of Montana's summer residents winter in western Mexico.**

While essential to the survival of birds, migration lends interest and color to all our lives. If migration ceased, we could no longer look forward to birds as harbingers of spring. No longer would the stranglehold of winter be broken by the sight of a wedge of whistling swans or the throes of cabin fever be snapped by the gabble of geese on a crisp moonlit night. As Aldo Leopold said in his book, *A Sand County Almanac,* "One swallow does not make a summer, but one skein of geese, cleaving the murk of a March thaw, is the spring."

a

b

c

# WINTER

Each winter wildlife suffers in a variety of ways. Waterfowl that haven't migrated die when ice covers their plant food, fish suffocate when lakes become so thickly covered with ice that oxygen supplies are cut off. Pheasants starve when their long tails become iced to the ground. Trout and salmon eggs are destroyed by the scouring action of ice. Deer and elk die when vegetation becomes insufficient to go around.

The wonder is that anything survives. But each spring brings a reawakening. There always remain embers of each species that have survived to reproduce their kind. Somehow they have made it through the toughest of seasons.

One of the most familiar means of survival is hibernation — a trancelike state that is the ultimate in energy conservation. Deep hibernators include the hoary marmot, a member of the woodchuck family, which in some parts of Montana sleeps away nine full months of its life each year. During this time the marmot's body temperature drops to just above freezing, its respiration rate becomes imperceptible, its heartbeat grows very faint and chemicals increase through the animal's system. These chemical changes improve the ability of the blood to clot, so a wound incurred during hibernation scarcely would bleed.

At this time death would result if the marmot's body temperature dropped below freezing. But, covered with thick fur, buried beneath dozens of feet of insulating

d

*Montana animals obviously are adapted for harsh winters, but for the weak and diseased, the very young and very old, and for the underfed, winter may be the cruelest population determinant. (a) Bighorn bedded down. (b) Elk breaking trail. (c) Squirrels in a cozy corner. (d) Black bear deep asleep in winter den.*

snow and having properly selected winter chambers, such deaths are infrequent.

Other animals get past winter by going into torpor, a state of sleep not quite as deep as hibernation. During this time the animal's body temperature remains close to normal, though breathing and circulation slow slightly. Creatures in this category include skunks, raccoons, and black and grizzly bears. And all are easily aroused, especially on mild days.

Many other warm-blooded animals subjected to extended periods of extreme cold will turn up their thermostats to regulate their metabolic furnaces. Fat reserves are burned faster for greater heat production. In contrast, the whitetail deer's metabolic regulator, the thyroid gland, actually slows body functions in winter. When food is scarce, energy consumption can be reduced to improve survival chances. This feature is unique to members of the deer family.

Coyotes and wolves fluff out their fur since their coats include hollow guard hairs that trap dead air close to the skin. Internal changes cause more blood to be pumped their paws, ears, tails and noses.

There are other ways of wintering. Frogs and turtles burrow into the mud bottoms. In spite of these ingenious adaptations, many creatures starve to death. Although it seems cruel, this process eliminates the weak and the sick and, in the long run, species are improved.

# RARE AND ENDANGERED SPECIES

## WOLVES

The wolf has been persecuted since white men first arrived in Montana. As a result there have been few confirmed sightings of wolves in the state since the 1940s.

In 1972, the Wolf Ecology Project, Missoula, began collecting information about tracks, and unconfirmed sightings have come from Lincoln County, the Sun River country, areas adjacent to Yellowstone National Park, the Gravelley range, and Valley County north of Glasgow.

In 1980 the Northern Rocky Mountain Wolf Recovery Plan was completed and a team of biologists, working under the auspices of the U.S. Fish and Wildlife Service, has been hoping to reestablish a viable population of wolves in Montana, Wyoming and Idaho.

## PEREGRINE FALCON

July 15, 1981 was the day of an historic event in Montana. On that day, a small box was opened and four young peregrine falcons were released into the wilds of Montana providing a bright spot for a species with an otherwise dismal future.

Like other rare and endangered species, peregrine falcon populations have declined because of habitat degradation. DDT and other pesticides contaminated its food, interfering with its reproductive success. The chemicals weaken egg shells to such an extent that the weight of the incubating female causes them to break. In addition, human activities encroached into their habitat, tipping the balance in favor of competing species.

Because of these problems, peregrine populations across the country have plummeted since the 1940s. In 1964, a noted ornithologist reported only 25 nesting pairs in Montana, an area containing 75 known eyries. By 1972, the number of active eyries had dropped to seven. No active eyries have been found since that time.

The events leading up to the momentous occasion of July 15, 1981, began several years ago with the formation of the Peregrine Fund, Inc. A private, nonprofit organization dedicated to the preservation of the peregrine and other birds of prey, the Fund began reintroducing peregrines produced in captivity into formerly occupied ranges.

The Fund maintains two breeding facilities, one at Cornell University in Ithaca, New York, and the other at Colorado State University, Fort Collins, Colorado. The Fort Collins facility expects to maintain production at more than 100 birds per year.

The eggs containing those peregrines destined for Montana, were produced by captive birds kept in heavily guarded enclosures and hatched in incubators. The hatchlings were hand fed by experts for the first few days before being placed with adult peregrines to receive imprinting, which is the psychological conditioning that enables young peregrines to recognize the facial pattern and behavior of other peregrines. Without imprinting, they do not know how to respond to others of their species, making it impossible for them to reproduce. After being kept at the Fort Collins site until they were 35 days old, the young birds were flown to the "hacking" site. Hacking refers to the gradual process of releasing a captive falcon into the wild.

The site was carefully chosen. Prior to releasing the birds the area was evaluated to assure ornithologists that the prospective release site contained not only an abundance of prey species but, moreover, that it was an area free from human disturbance and was one having few potential predators.

For 10 days prior to the release, the falcons were confined to a hack box, specially constructed to allow the falcons to see out and adjust to their surroundings. During this time, the precious peregrines were under the almost constant supervision of dedicated caretakers who guarded and fed them. Finally on July 15, the front of the hack box was removed, and the fledglings faced the real world for the first time.

Carrying radio transmitters, the birds were under constant surveillance until August 20, 1981. On that date, the caretakers departed and the young birds were truly on their own.

More releases are planned and because of successes with this method in other areas, the peregrine may have a future in Montana.

# WHOOPING CRANES

Montana's other rare and endangered bird, the whooping crane, does not breed in the state. Dedicated or lucky observers may see these birds as they pass through eastern Montana in spring or fall on their way from their wintering grounds on the Texas Gulf coast to their remote breeding grounds on the Sass River in Wood Buffalo National Park, Northwest Territories, Canada.

Never numerous, the numbers of whooping cranes diminished with the takeover of marshes by cities, agriculture and summer-home developments. Whoopers decreased to a low of 14 birds in 1938. Through protection of their remaining habitat, propagation of captive birds, and projects using adopted sandhill crane parents to raise whooping crane chicks, it appears that whooping cranes will remain for the enjoyment of future generations.

# BLACK-FOOTED FERRET

Black-footed ferrets are among the rarest and least understood mammals in the state. In fact, their presence in the state is questionable. The last specimen was a road kill collected near Alzada, in Carter County, in November of 1953. Since then, only one authentic observation has been recorded.

The plains Indians had many superstitions and ceremonies commemorating these ferrets, evidence that they always were rare. Still, between 1919 and 1928, government trappers in Montana took 18 ferrets, an indication that they were more numerous at that time than they are today.

Inhabitants of prairie dog towns, ferrets are about the size of mink. They are brownish-yellow with a distinctive black face mask. The last third of the tail and their feet are also jet black. Nocturnal and secretive, they rarely venture out during the day.

*(a) Many believe the peregrine falcon to be the most beautiful, if rapacious, of the raptors. Certainly it is the most threatened, but new releases hold hope for a truly wild population.*

Short of seeing ferrets, informed observers might detect their presence by sign. During the process of modifying a prairie dog burrow for their own use, ferrets often form a trench-like structure in the mound, and, while prarie dogs use the dirt to build up a dome-like mound, black-footed ferrets usually scatter it beyond the mound. Also, since prairie dogs are known to plug burrows occupied by ferrets or other predators, the presence of several plugged burrows in a town may indicate a ferret.

Because they depend on prairie dog colonies for their survival, authorities agree that the only way to manage ferrets is to manage prairie dog colonies. Poisoning prairie dogs is the reason for the decline of these unique animals and, unless carefully controlled, will seal their doom.

"The last word in ignorance is the man who says of an animal or plant: 'What good is it?' If the land mechanism as a whole is good, then every part is good, whether we understand it or not."

Aldo Leopold from *A Sand County Almanac*

## About Our Back Cover Photo
This photographic mosaic was compiled from Earth Resources Satellite Photo passes made from a height of 570 miles. It was pieced together in black and white and interpreted in color by Big Sky Magic, Larry Dodge, Owner.
Commercial Color Adaptation © 1976 Big Sky Magic.

This series fills the need for in-depth information about Montana subjects. The geographic concept explores the historic color, the huge landscape and the resilient people of a single subject or area. Design by Len Visual Design, Helena, Montana. Color lithography by Dai Nippon, San Francisco. Printed in Japan. All camera prep work and layout production completed in Helena, Montana. Typesetting by Thurber Printing, Helena, Montana.

# PHOTO CREDITS

**Front Cover**
*Eagle — Alan Carey*
*Bull Elk — Michael Quinton*
*Pelicans — Rodney Krey*
*Flying Squirrel — Jan Wassink*
*Tanager — Jan Wassink*
*Mountain Goats — Rick Hoerner*

**Preface — Contents Pages**
*Fox — Tim Christie*
*Ibis — Jan Wassink*
*Wolverine — Alan Carey*
*Grizzly Bear — Alan Carey*
*Raccoon — Alan Carey*
*Hummingbird — Bert Gildart*
*Elk — Alan Carey*
*Lynx — Tom Ulrich*
*Ring-necked Pheasant — Tom Ulrich*
*Bison — Mike Sample*
*Mountain Goat — Bert Gildart*

**Lincoln Allen:** *113e*
**Pete & Alice Bengeyfield:** *102c, 103b, 109b, 109c*
**Alan Carey:** *38b, 38c, 42a, 44a, 45, 48, 55a, 59a, 64a, 66a, 66c, 70a, 74b, 74c, 77d, 79c, 79d, 81a, 82a, 84, 88a, 89, 92c, 93a, 95b, 95c, 95g, 97d, 100b, 103a, 103c, 104a, 104b, 104h, 105e, 106a, 106b, 107a, 107b, 108d, 109d, 114e, 120c*
**Jon Cates:** *76c, 80c, 104f*
**Doug Chadwick:** *47*
**Tim Christie:** *15d, 24b, 25a, 32a, 32b, 33d, 44d, 77b, 79e, 97b, 108b, 109a*
**Bob Cooney:** *13a, 13c*
**Kristi DuBois:** *27*
**Neil Duke:** *62c*
**Phil Farnes:** *54c, 56c, 105a, 121a, 121b, 121c*
**Michael Francis:** *54b, 56b, 68b*
**Bert Gildart:** *10, 11, 12a, 12b, 14, 15a, 15c, 16a, 19b, 19d, 20b, 21a, 21b, 23a, 23b, 25b, 25c, 33c, 34a, 35a, 35b, 36a, 36b, 37a, 39b, 44b, 50a, 50b, 52b, 53, 55b, 59b, 60a, 62b, 63b, 67, 74a, 76a, 76b, 79a, 81b, 92a, 97i, 98a, 98c, 98d, 99g, 101b, 101h, 104d, 104g, 105f, 106c, 107e, 109e, 110c, 110d, 118a, 118b, 118c, 118d, 119a, 120a, 122a, 124, 125, 126*
**Charles E. Kay:** *22a, 37d, 37e, 38a, 88b, 88c, 122b*
**Rodney Krey:** *18, 99d*
**Paul Lally:** *68c*
**Jan Mack:** *36c*
**Tim Milburn:** *92d*
**Neal Mishler:** *42b, 75b, 90b, 113l, 114b*
**Courtesy of Montana Historical Society:** *4, 6, 7, 8, 9*
**Tom Murphy:** *115a*
**Doug O'looney:** *87a*
**Barb & Mike Pflaum:** *49*
**Wayne Scherr:** *20a*
**Tracy Scott:** *64b*
**Mike Quinton:** *19a, 28a, 28c, 37c, 41a, 43, 65, 87b, 91d, 95d, 123a*
**Michael Sample:** *12c, 40, 42d, 46a, 46c, 50c, 57, 71a, 85, 86, 95a, 96a, 119b, 119c, 123b, 123d*
**Tom Ulrich:** *22b, 29a, 30b, 30c, 31a, 31c, 37b, 41b, 68a, 75c, 77a, 80a, 82c, 90a, 90c, 92b, 97c, 97e, 97f, 97h, 97j, 97l, 99a, 99b, 99h, 99i, 100a, 100c, 100d, 100e, 101a, 101c, 101d, 101e, 101f, 101g, 104e, 108c, 112a, 113c, 113g, 113m, 113n, 113p, 113q, 114a, 114c, 114d, 115b*
**Courtesy, University of Montana Archives, Elrod Collection:** *16b, 17*
**Jan Wassink:** *15b, 19c, 24a, 30a, 31b, 31d, 33a, 33b, 34c, 39a, 42c, 44c, 46b, 51a, 51b, 51c, 52a, 54a, 56a, 58, 59c, 61, 62a, 63a, 69, 70b, 70c, 71b, 71c, 71d, 72a, 72b, 73, 79b, 83d, 93b, 94, 95e, 95f, 96b, 97a, 97g, 98b, 99c, 99e, 100f, 102a, 102b, 103d, 104c, 105b, 105c, 105d, 107c, 107d, 108a, 110a, 110b, 111a, 111b, 111c, 111d, 113a, 113b, 113d, 113f, 113h, 113i, 113j, 113k, 113o, 114f, 116a, 116b, 117a, 117b, 117c, 117d, 117e, 117f, 119d, 120b, 123a, 123c, 123d, 123e*
**Ed Wolff:** *66b, 77c, 82b*
**George Wuerthner:** *13b, 28b, 29b, 29c, 34b, 60b, 75a, 80b, 91a, 91b, 91c, 97k, 99f*